FROM A SPEAKEASY TO THE CROSS

FROM A SPEAKEASY TO THE CROSS
A CHRISTIAN'S STORY

REV.DR.CLIFFORD
E.
BAKER

Pleasant Word
A Division of WINEPRESS PUBLISHING

© 2006 by The Rev. Dr. Clifford Baker. All rights reserved.

Pleasant Word (a division of WinePress Publishing, PO Box 428, Enumclaw, WA 98022) functions only as book publisher. As such, the ultimate design, content, editorial accuracy, and views expressed or implied in this work are those of the author.

No part of this publication may be reproduced, stored in a retrieval system or transmitted in any way by any means—electronic, mechanical, photocopy, recording or otherwise—without the prior permission of the copyright holder, except as provided by USA copyright law.

Unless otherwise noted, all Scriptures are taken from the Holy Bible, New International Version, Copyright © 1973, 1978, 1984 by the International Bible Society. Used by permission of Zondervan Publishing House. The "NIV" and "New International Version" trademarks are registered in the United States Patent and Trademark Office by International Bible Society.

Scripture references marked KJV are taken from the King James Version of the Bible.

Scripture references marked NASB are taken from the New American Standard Bible, © 1960, 1963, 1968, 1971, 1972, 1973, 1975, 1977 by The Lockman Foundation. Used by permission.

ISBN 1-4141-0505-3
Library of Congress Catalog Card Number: 2005904670

DEDICATION

This book is dedicated to the memories of three men
who were my surrogate fathers
in my younger years
after my own father died.

The first was my Captain in the U.S. Navy, Captain Delavough.
He sent me from one island invasion to the next,
yet he always said that I would come back alive
and, after the war, that I would attend college.

The second was the Rev. Dr. Jesse Hays Baird.
He was president of San Francisco Theological Seminary
in San Anselmo during the years I attended.
When I got into trouble, he would place his arm around me
and say,
"You are going to be a sawdust trail evangelist
just like I was."

The third of these men was the Rev. Dr. James Earl Jackman, secretary for the National Board of Missions of the United Presbyterian Church.
When I graduated from seminary and was unable to find a call he assured me that God would always find a place for me.
Dr. Jackman was really my Bishop!

TABLE OF CONTENTS

Chapter 1: Guam 9
Chapter 2: A Lonely Swim 15
Chapter 3: Nearly Captured 21
Chapter 4: Jamming Radio Signals 25
Chapter 5: I'll Never Go Again! 29
Chapter 6: "If I Don't Come Back…" 33
Chapter 7: The Church 37
Chapter 8: The War Continues 41
Chapter 9: The Persian Gulf 49
Chapter 10: Speakeasies 53
Chapter 11: The Neighborhood 57
Chapter 12: The Fountain Family 59
Chapter 13: You're in the Navy Now! 63
Chapter 14: I Need a Volunteer 69
Chapter 15: You Don't Want to Know! 73
Chapter 16: Choices 75
Chapter 17: President Roosevelt's Prayer 81
Chapter 18: Ask Cliff to Preach 87
Chapter 19: A Real Job Offer? Bah! 91
Chapter 20: Seminary 95

Chapter 21: Turkey Shoot 101
Chapter 22: Fire Danger!..105
Chapter 23: "Fifteen Two! Fifteen Four!"...109
Chapter 24: Sneaking a Peek 113
Chapter 25: Fight or Run, Preacher!..115
Chapter 26: Easter Surprise 119
Chapter 27: An Offer to Leave 123
Chapter 28: New Church Development..125
Chapter 29: A Vision of Jesus..127
Chapter 30: Merging Presbyterians and Baptists............................129
Chapter 31: A Serpent in the Garden of Eden 133
Chapter 32: Dr. James Earl Jackman Rides to My Rescue.............137
Chapter 33: Hell's Angels and Hot Dogs..141
Chapter 34: Disadvantages of Being Clergy...................................145
Chapter 35: The Cellar..149
Chapter 36: Millwright Carpenter..151
Chapter 37: The Holy Spirit Always Finds a Way..........................153
Chapter 38: The Mill Bible 157
Chapter 39: McCloud Centennial...161

CHAPTER ONE

GUAM

The submarine gently nosed its way upward until it came to rest just below the surface. It lay nearly motionless about a mile off the west coastline of Guam. Only the sub's conning tower was poking ever so slightly out of the shimmering sea. The submarine was deep inside enemy-occupied territory. Prior to breaching, the sub's commanding officer had carefully scanned surrounding waves and sky with his periscope for any telltale signs of Japanese patrol boats or spotter aircraft.

Down in the sub's bowels, I gathered up all of my gear and started a short climb straight up a narrow ladder inside the conning tower. Once the hatch was screwed open, I gasped a long, deep breath of fresh sea air. The salt stung my lungs as a bit of spray hit me in the face. Although it tasted a bit like the salty mouth of the mighty Columbia River back home, I was half a world away from the rough-and-tumble speakeasy—an illegal hard liquor and gambling establishment—that my parents operated in Washington State.

And, as a self-confessed atheist, I was heading even further away from the cross that would eventually redeem my life and give it purpose, meaning and everlasting salvation.

It was the evening of July 15, 1944.

From a Speakeasy to the Cross

The sub captain had timed our arrival precisely to coincide with the first few moments of sunset. He placed his vessel directly in a line between the island's closest observers and the sun's distant glowing orb that was even now beginning to sink below the watery horizon.

I was preparing to go ashore on Guam, alone and behind enemy lines.

My one and only job—besides trying to stay alive—was to jam Japanese radio transmissions for five days leading up to an Allied invasion. U.S. Marines, assisted by forces from New Zealand and Australia, would soon make an assault on the beach in an effort to retake the strategically located island. Guam had once served as an important outpost for the U.S. military. If the pending invasion succeeded, Guam would once again play a pivotal role in what we all hoped would ultimately lead to Japan's defeat.

Things were heating up again in the Pacific Theater of World War II.

Just five weeks before, Europe witnessed the dramatic invasion of Normandy on June 6. There, the blood of thousands of America's bravest fighting men was spilled on the beaches and mingled with that of British and Canadian forces. Each country suffered heavy losses while assaulting Nazi German gun emplacements and troops.

On June 14, just eight days after D-Day commenced, U.S. Marines also waded ashore at Tinian in the Marianas Islands. Those Marines were practically within spitting distance of Japan itself. But most Americans and fewer Europeans were ever made aware of the war actions taking place on the world's other side.

Neither the troops dug into foxholes on the battle lines nor sailors asleep in their bunks on ships at sea knew it yet, but Allied commanders had been meeting in secret for weeks. They were planning a massive invasion just six days hence. The plan pivoted on the retaking of Guam. And they expected heavy resistance from members of Japan's 320th Independent Infantry Battalion, as well as the men of Japan's 1st Battalion, 38th Infantry, which had been in possession of the island for nearly three years.

Before the U.S. Marines could go ashore on Guam with bombs and guns blazing, my orders were to swim ashore alone. Days ahead of

Guam

any armed invasion force, it would be my job to create enough radio interference to hamper an extensive Japanese communications network. If left intact, Japanese radio operators on Guam might too easily call for reinforcements. They also could tip off commanding officers regarding future invasions planned for other Japanese-held islands in the same region.

I was one of nearly 200 U.S. Navy volunteers—either radio technicians or other specialists—who secretly trained for our next landing. We were all stationed at Iroquois Point on the Hawaiian Island of Oahu. Today, Iroquois Point is a sleepy subdivision just west of Honolulu. During the war, however, its strategic position at the western mouth of Pearl Harbor proved ideal for training Special Operations forces. We didn't know it then, but our Special Operations unit would eventually spawn what is today the U.S. Navy Seals.

Despite our intense training prior to this mission, I was scared of capture, torture and death at the hands of enemy soldiers. My active imagination had the Japanese Army populating every inch of Guam's 212 square miles. From my perch on the conning mast of that attack submarine, I could just make out the rocks, sand beaches and jungle-covered hillsides beckoning cruelly across the waves. My assigned landing area was just south of Oka Point. I was soon to learn that this was a mixed sand and rock beach forming Agana Bay. What little I could see of Guam at this moment, however, was brilliantly lit with hues of lost gold, burnt orange and blood red in the last rays of a rapidly setting sun.

But this wasn't a time to sightsee.

During the first of what would eventually be my seven landings of which only three were pre-invasion. I was to make every mistake possible and yet survive to tell the tale some sixty-one years later.

In preparation for my swim ashore, my orders were to commit to memory a map of the entire island. Along with a general sense of Guam's coastline, I also was supposed to know exact locations of specific hills that my mission commanders had sequentially numbered. Special Operations personnel were not allowed to carry along any papers or official records of any kind when engaged in radio jamming sorties. We didn't even wear dog tags, the metal identification pieces that all other soldiers wore. This was done to prevent torture in case of capture by the enemy, our trainers said.

I was selected as a radio jammer out of boot camp partly because I had bragged about having a fantastic memory. But photographic recall wasn't one of my skills! Now, suddenly, I was supposed to absorb and internalize the map of an entire island. Drawing and art classes had always been a problem for me during school and growing up in Vancouver, Wash. I could neither draw a map of Guam nor memorize the map.

Studying the map and hill locations, I drew a series of straight lines between them. Connecting the lines caused various geometric shapes to emerge. Unlike art, mathematics has always been easy for me. Remembering numbered points on a triangle, rectangle, rhombus or other shape is much easier than remembering a series of map coordinates.

Each corner of the geometric shapes represented one of the hilltops from which I was to observe the enemy encampments, receive supplies, or jam Japanese radio transmissions. Each hilltop had an assigned number, usually between one and 12. As a jammer I was supposed to climb an unoccupied hilltop for a brief period of time. From there, we would try to block portions of any Japanese messages being transmitted or received.

Early on in World War II, the Japanese military set up a massive network of observation outposts stringing together hundreds of islands throughout the western Pacific Ocean. Radio provided the linkage. From these multiple watching and listening posts, enemy soldiers could easily track U.S. and allied naval and air force movements. My job was to create only enough interference so the Japanese would be unable to complete their messages. It was not possible to halt all communication by the enemy. To do my task without getting caught, I was trained to move from hilltop to hilltop at irregular intervals throughout my uninvited stay on the island. That way, if the Japanese tried to use directional finders, theoretically I would be long gone by the time they reached my last detected position.

A British commando I knew as "Limey" (English) told me during one pre-invasion training exercise that no matter what my official orders were, my real job was always to stay alive! Even if that sometimes meant disobeying orders.

Guam

His instructions suited my rebellious attitude just fine. All of the training we received on swimming ashore undetected, eliminating enemy soldier patrols and jamming radio signals was to help us avoid capture, the Limey commando told each of us more than once.

Our instructors always used the word "capture" rather than suggest any of us might somehow be killed for our actions. In reality, of the 200 specialists who were trained in my amphibious unit, only two of us survived the entire war as far as I know.

World War II Special Forces, Amphibious Assault unit members "Socks" Rodgers, upper left, "Lucky" Cliff Baker (author), upper center "Sully" Joe Sullivan, upper right, "Slick," lower right. Among nearly 200 radio technicians and operators similarly trained for special operations, only "Lucky" and "Slick" survived the war.

Another reason for memorizing the numbered hilltops: U.S. Navy spotter aircraft could air drop supplies and additional equipment too bulky or heavy for a man to carry on a solo swim ashore. The planes were similar in looks and size to a piper cub. They would fly over an island—again coming from the west just at sunset to better avoid detection by the Japanese. Signals made with the radio jamming equipment could let U.S. Navy pilots know which hilltop was free of the enemy. Once the parachuted supplies were successfully retrieved, I then would have radio monitoring equipment and more than a day's supply of food.

If the Japanese were somewhere between me and a hilltop, or if the Japanese had stationed an outpost there, a Morse Code "N" signal would indicate a No Drop. The spotter pilot and jammer would then move to a hilltop with the next higher number for another try.

In addition to remembering the relative locations and numbers of each hilltop, we also were required to memorize each radio frequency used by the Japanese. These frequencies were detected by U.S. Navy submarines surfacing at night. A radio technician on each submarine would jam a particular frequency. When the enemy switched frequencies, the sub would scan all radio frequencies to locate the new transmission frequency.

It was a natural tendency in those early days of two-way radio communication to use primary frequency, but then to have several others as secondary alternatives. An operator would move to a different frequency only if the signal was jammed. However, radio operators can't just switch to any random frequency since the person on the other end of the transmission also must use the same frequency to hear and send messages. Everyone operated off a list. After all, if there is no way to communicate, how else could the receiving operator know which frequency to try next?

CHAPTER TWO

A LONELY SWIM

Allied forces were scheduled to make a landing July 21, 1944, on Guam and retake the island. I swam ashore alone from a surfaced submarine on the evening of July 15, just as the sun was setting. Mission planners concluded that any Japanese sentry on beach patrol would be unable to look directly into the setting sun. That is one of the many ways I escaped detection.

The submarine surfaced about a mile off shore, as much to avoid being seen as to avoid any coral reefs ringing the island. Using the submarine's conning tower as cover, I entered the water on the side farthest away from the island. But before I could make my approach to the beach I waited a few moments as the submarine sailed ahead a short distance before starting its descent far beneath the surface.

Now, I truly was alone.

I was scared to death when I finally entered the dark blue Pacific waters. Since Guam is so near the equator, the sea temperature was not cold. But as I was heading toward a strange island filled with enemy soldiers, it was very frightening!

Staying about fifteen to twenty feet below the water's surface, I used my swim fins and the ocean surge for extra propulsion as I traveled nearly a mile fully submerged. Whenever the ocean pushed me forward, my ankles would tilt to a 90-degree angle and allow the swim fins to hang straight down. In this position, my fins acted like miniature sails. The ocean surge propelled me along until the back flow started pushing against me from the other direction. At that point, tension would release in my ankles, my knees would bend and a few kicks of my legs would propel me forward until another surge started. By repeating these methods in rhythm with the ocean surges I was able to cover the entire distance without expending too much energy.

But I took my time, partly to let the sun go down so that darkness would hide my coming actions. Close to the equator it gets dark very rapidly, especially when there are no shore lights to brighten the sky.

On each of my three swims ashore, I wore what was called a dry suit. I wriggled into it feet first through an opening in the chest area. Then I pulled on the suit's upper part over my shoulders, arms and head. Once securely inside, the suit's extra material around the chest opening was twisted, then tied shut. Done properly, this kept any sea water out. The heavy, rubberized suit had a face hole which was covered with a glass-plated diving mask. That way, I could see while swimming underwater. Wrist and ankle holes allowed my hands and feet to protrude from the suit. On my bare feet I wore black rubber fins boldly stamped "U.S. Navy." On one wrist I wore a depth gauge, and on the other a waterproof watch.

Under the dry suit, I wore a set of cotton long-johns—both top and bottom—to wick up any perspiration. Long-johns also prevented the loosely-fitting rubber suit from sticking to my skin. Some of the other amphibious assault specialists wore wool long johns for extra warmth. But wool makes me itch.

Over the chest area of my dry suit, I strapped a rubberized canvas yoke—an extra, portable lung—called a rebreather. Compressed air tanks and other S.C.U.B.A. equipment had not yet been invented. But the U.S. Navy had been using deep water diving helmets and breathing hoses attached to pumps for years. Rebreathers were the Navy's first attempt at a portable breathing device. They were only good for very shallow dives since they supplied bottled oxygen that was mixed together with exhaled air. An air hose connected the chest bag to my mask.

A Lonely Swim

The rebreather allowed me to breath underwater while preventing any telltale bubbles from rising to the surface.

Each time I exhaled, a small charcoal filter would remove most of the carbon dioxide from my closed air supply. Whenever the rebreather bag air got too stale, I simply opened a valve briefly to release small amounts of pure oxygen into the rebreather bag. The oxygen came from a small tank strapped across my chest. The rebreathers worked pretty well, but we couldn't dive very deep as oxygen poisoning sets in at just below 30 feet.

My boots, socks and combat uniform, along with a day's supply of emergency rations and my all-important little radio contact equipment went into a waterproof cargo bag called a "trailer." The trailer bag was strapped to a webbed and weighted belt also worn on the outside of the dry suit. I preferred my trailer bag to hung loose around my knees when I swam so it would not interfere with the movement of my hands or legs.

The webbed belt had a series of lead weights attached to it. All Special Operations personal were meticulous in attaching enough lead on their belt so the combined weight would offset any natural buoyancy of the body, dry suit and rebreather equipment. That way we didn't have to struggle at staying below the surface as we swam.

We had enough other things to think about.

The weight belt was also handy when nearing a beach. Once a jammer got close enough for his feet to touch bottom, he would remove his mask, flippers and rebreather equipment. The weighted belt anchored the trailer bag and all gear on the shallow ocean bottom until it was retrieved. The only weapon I carried ashore was a K-Bar knife strapped to my right leg. I always wore it where my right hand could easily reach it.

The most important piece of equipment in my trailer bag, however, was a small hand-held radio static transmitter. It was to signal the observation plane. The device was about the size and shape of those counting clickers that some sports arena gate attendants carry. Unlike the counters, however, it had inside a wheel that spins rapidly whenever the thumb button is pressed. The mechanism generates static on whatever radio frequency it is set.

Close to shore, I dropped off my equipment, took one last breath from the rebreather bag, and rose slowly to the water's surface. I was careful not to make any sudden moves. Sounds of the surf gently washing onto the beach helped hide any noise.

Slowly, and very gradually, I raised my forehead, eyes and nose just above the water line until I could once again breath and see. If anyone had been watching, I must have resembled nothing more dangerous than a sea turtle. Just my eyeballs and nostrils poked out of the water. Seeing nothing at first, I began to relax. Then I noticed the faint but unmistakable smell of tobacco smoke. I learned later, after completing several other jamming raids, that nearly all of the Japanese beach patrols were heavy smokers.

That was good for me because I could smell burning tobacco from quite a distance. Usually, if I was close enough, I could even see the glow of a Japanese sentry's cigarette butt as he inhaled.

Nearly submerged, I waited quietly in the water as a beach sentry walked past my position. I was still about 30 yards away from dry sand, but I could watch unseen everything that moved on the beach.

Even after the sentry passed by, I continued to wait in the gently rolling surf. Using my waterproof watch to time his actions, I needed to know how frequently the patrols passed this particular spot. It seemed like an eternity before the sentry returned for another pass. That second time, I was prepared for quick action.

I swam as close to the sandiest portion of the mixed rock and sand beach as I could find while still lying covered mostly by the water. After the Japanese sentry walked by me the second time, I slipped up behind him as quietly as a big cat.

Taking prisoners was out of the question. So I weighed the only option remaining to me and slit his throat. At that moment, it was either him or me. And I wanted to remain alive. Growing up I found myself in quite a few school, neighborhood and bar fights, but this Japanese soldier was the first person I had ever killed.

I did it just as we had been trained. Heading back into the water, I used the dead soldier's own helmet to carry water back to where his body lay. I washed away any signs of blood on the sand. After retrieving my trailer bag from where it lay on the bottom of the shallow bay, I then

A Lonely Swim

put the dead sentry's boots on my own feet. That way, any footprints on the beach would look like his. Dragging the dead soldier and all of my gear up the sand to the jungle's edge was my next chore.

I found a small ravine where I hid the body. I covered the corpse with jungle brush. The Japanese sentry was a small man. Whatever the size, dead bodies are still quite awkward to move. Dragging him across the sand had left some deep tracks. Using a section of leafy brush, I wiped out all tracks on the beach, especially mine.

The rapidly darkening night air was hot and sticky with humidity. There wasn't much else to do. Not wanting to be surprised by another beach patrol looking for the missing sentry, I searched for a likely place to spend what remained of the night. At last, after all other preparations were completed, I climbed a small hill nearby.

My assigned landing spot was at about Guam's midpoint. The southern end of the island is covered with steep hills and deep valleys while the northern half is more gently rolling grassland. Where I landed, however, there wasn't a lot of open area. It was mostly jungle with just enough space between the vegetation to slip through.

CHAPTER THREE

NEARLY CAPTURED

Several mistakes were made on my first landing, and I was lucky to get back alive.

As careful as I thought I had been, I look back on it now and realize it was a very hurried job. Since Guam was my first commando experience, I thought my efforts looked pretty good. Afterwards, I climbed a nearby hill and found a place where I could get some rest.

Before I fell asleep, however, I buried my swimming gear and covered the area with jungle debris. I quickly changed into my combat uniform and put on my own boots. I was tired from the swim ashore, my encounter with the enemy soldier, and the exertion required to move his dead body off the beach and bury it. Sleep came slowly, but finally I got some needed rest.

I awoke suddenly to the sounds of someone shouting in Japanese on the same beach where I had waded ashore just hours before.

Not wanting to be spotted, I carefully raised my head just enough to get a glimpse of the beach below. There stood a group of soldiers. One officer was pointing to the ground and shouting something at the others in Japanese.

Quickly making a mental checklist, I wondered what could have been left behind on the beach to alert the Japanese. Could it be that one of my swim fins had dropped onto the sand? Maybe something had drifted ashore before retrieval of the trailer bag. I'll never know because I didn't stick around to find out. Enemy patrols were already looking for me. Even as I prepared to evacuate the hilltop, sounds of Japanese soldiers scrambling through underbrush drew ever closer to my position.

As a very young boy growing up in Vancouver, Wash., my grandmother—a full-blooded Oglalla Sioux—trained me in the Indian ways. One of the earliest survival skills she drilled into me was the nature position to escape detection or danger. Looking quickly around, I found a good hiding place with lots of ground cover. I took a deep breath and curled up while lying on my side.

I do not know how long I lay motionless and undetected in the nature position that particular time on Guam. When I finally returned from the meditative state, the sun was high overhead. The Japanese soldiers had also departed without finding me.

I was relieved to still be alive, even though I wonder to this day what it was that I had done or left undone to alert them that an intruder was on the island.

The nature position or fetal position is one step towards entering a meditative state. The trance-like condition that all Indian boys learn, according to my grandmother, is brought on by closing both eyes and repeatedly thinking about lying in your mother's arms as an infant. A feeling of warmth and safety envelops the practitioner. There is no fear, anger or aggressiveness in you when in the nature position. Only after all danger is gone does one come out of the meditative state. Although the practitioner is often deep in a trance for up to several hours, very often he will still remember things that happened to or around him during that disconnected time period.

My first experience of really needing the nature position happened when I was still a small boy. I had wandered up the creek away from where my family was camping. I saw a bear scooping fish out of the water with just her claws. Then I heard a noise behind me. When I turned a little to my left, I could see and hear a bear cub crying.

Realizing immediately that I was standing between the mother bear and her mewling cub, I went into the nature position after taking a

Nearly Captured

deep breath. When I came out of the meditative state as a young boy, I remember the bear brushing my skin and clothing as she ran by me to reach her cub. To her, the curled up ball I had become was no more a threat than any other stump or piece of brush.

On Guam, it wasn't a bear that scared me. It was the Japanese army. When I finally came out of the nature position on Guam, I waited for at least an hour but there were no more sounds of any enemy soldiers surrounding me or my hillside. I lay quietly, just listening for a long, long time with my eyes closed. My grandmother had also taught me, "No matter how quiet you are, if you open your eyes they will find you. The eyes are a path."

At one time or another, everyone has felt as if someone was staring at them from behind. When that happens and the person turns around, very often he or she will see the eyes of another person staring back. As my grandmother often reminded me, remember always that the eyes are a path!

CHAPTER FOUR

JAMMING RADIO SIGNALS

Throughout that first day, I made my way with great difficulty through the island jungle. First, I climbed a hilltop from where I hoped to be able to locate a group of even taller hilltops that I remembered as the points of a triangle. My ultimate objective was to locate hilltop No. 1 on my mental map. That is where a U.S. Navy observation plane would soon drop my survival rations, extra clothing and radio monitoring equipment.

I was able to follow a few animal trails through the thick jungle brush, but only for short distances. Since the wild animals were much smaller than I, this method of travel involved a lot of crawling. I also remember that the jungle brush was pretty scratchy in spots. At other times in my traversing the island, I was surprised to discover that there were almost no plants covering the ground except for some tall grasses.

I finally reached hilltop No. 1 where I waited for the sunset. That was when I knew to expect the U.S. Navy observation plane. It would fly over and make a drop if I signaled that the area was clear of Japanese.

The U.S. Navy used a small, light plane that resembled a Piper Cub. Small planes were used because they were able to turn so quickly that a Japanese fighter plane could not follow it. But because spotter planes were slow, they were particularly susceptible to anti-aircraft guns fired from the ground. That is why the U.S. Navy pilots were so careful not to fly over too much of an island. If they stayed over the ocean, then it appeared to the Japanese just like a submarine scouting flight.

After what seemed like another eternity, the U.S. Navy observation plane came flying directly at my position from its hiding place in the rays of the setting sun. I quickly signaled a short burst of static, then a longer burst for the Morse Code letter "A," which indicated "Yes." That way, the pilot knew is was safe to drop my supplies and equipment. The small parachutes were released on the side of the hill farthest away from any Japanese positions. But the thick jungle brush and trees snagged the chutes and I had a terrible time getting to all of it. If sent a long and a short "N" that meant we will try the next hill.

I had no choice of leaving anything behind, however. I needed everything that the plane dropped. If I left so much as a parachute or nylon rope in the trees, it was sure to be spotted the next time a Japanese foot or aerial patrol passed through the area. The good news was I now had more rations and some radio monitoring equipment. Finally, I could tell when and how long the Japanese were transmitting messages to other islands.

The second day on Guam was spent monitoring Japanese radio signals. I was waiting for their messages to get longer and more frequent. Once that happened, I would use the top secret jamming device to create interference.

To the receiving party, the interference is a rasping sound much like the noise of a motor left running too closely to a poorly insulated radio. The transmitting party could not hear anything unless another Japanese soldier on the island was monitoring the same signal. That was highly unlikely, I thought.

When the receiving party eventually signaled back that they had been unable to receive the entire message, both sender and receiver switched to the next frequency on their lists. I searched my memory and switched over as well to follow them. Everything was going according to plan except I forgot one important part of my training. Guam was my first pre-invasion special operation experience, and so I made my second—and this time nearly fatal—mistake.

By now, the Japanese soldiers all knew that an uninvited intruder most likely was on the island with them. While I was busy jamming their

Jamming Radio Signals

longer transmissions, others apparently were busy using their radio location finders to pinpoint the hilltop source of the signal interference.

I had overstayed my welcome, but it was now too late for me to move to another hilltop. By the time I realized what was happening, Japanese soldiers were whistling to each other from all around my position. And the sounds of their advancement were rapidly moving closer to my somewhat exposed position. Higher hilltops in the tropics often have less jungle brush on them because they are regularly scoured bare by strong winds and large tropical storms, called typhoons, which meander through the Pacific.

Hide! My brain screamed at me. But there were few good places to do so. Finally, I covered all of my radio equipment and other gear with my body. Taking a deep breath, once again I went into the nature position taught to me by my Indian grandmother.

Closing my eyes tightly and silently repeating over and over the thoughts that would bring on a meditative state, my mind filled with a single thought: "I am lying in my mother's arms. She is nursing me. The sun is shining. And the temperature is warm."

It didn't matter if I was freezing cold at midnight surrounded by Japanese soldiers intent on finding me and putting an end to my life. As long as I was in the nature position, I felt safe and secure in my mother's arms. No danger could possibly touch me.

Although I was meditating and silent, almost in a transcendental state, my mind was still registering what was happening all around me. However, it wasn't until after I came out of the trance that those memories could be recalled.

As clearly as I can hear the sound of my wife's voice today, I remember a Japanese officer shouting out in perfect English at the ever-moving shadows of a tropical jungle night:

"I can see you in there. Come out with your hands up and I will not let my men bayonet you!" he yelled.

It was a bluff, of course!

No one could see me huddled over my equipment among the bushes. Still in a meditative state, I lay motionless with my breathing slowed and my eyes closed. I did not move nor respond. And that is what saved my life for the second time in just three days.

Hours later—I cannot tell you how long I lay in the nature position until my body realized that the danger had passed—I started to breath regularly again and was able to stretch out. But I kept my eyes closed for quite a while longer.

Thinking back on that experience today, I realize that some Japanese officers were attending school at colleges and universities in the United States prior to the start of hostilities in the Pacific theater. Months later I was to learn that a few of them had even been enrolled at California State University, Berkeley. Most of the Japanese educated in this country could speak English better than I could.

My remaining two days on Guam passed without further serious incident until just before the invasion started. Since I knew the exact date and time the invasion was to begin, I started making my own preparations the day before. I dug a deep foxhole within a hundred yards of the beach. This way, any artillery shells lobbed onto the island from the advancing Allied ships were supposed to sail safely over my head.

Not all of them did, of course! Every once in a while I could hear one of the large shells fall far short of its target further inland. But the foxhole protected me.

Once the American troops landed and came ashore to establish a beachhead, then came the most dangerous part of my entire mission. Coming from behind enemy lines, I had to cross through both the Japanese and the American battlefronts to reach my communications section. That is where I could expect to find any evacuation orders.

It was easy to slip by the Japanese, but remember that I wasn't carrying any identification or paper orders. All of my orders were memorized. And I had to identify myself to be allowed in by the American sentries. Sometimes, to keep from being shot by my own side, I had to cuss the sentries out and answer silly questions before it was safe enough for me to stand up and cross over.

Even when I had the correct passwords memorized for that particular day, the passwords often did me no good. The passwords were made nearly useless because too many American sentries had been tricked by English-speaking Japanese soldiers. For this reason, many American sentries had a policy of: "Shoot first, ask questions later."

CHAPTER FIVE
I'LL NEVER GO AGAIN!

Because I was a "jammer," the U.S. Navy pulled me off of Guam and flew me back to Hawaii just a few days after the invasion began.

On that first return to my staging area, I was so mad at the skipper, Captain Delavough, that I stormed into his office and began cussing him out. I told him I would be more than happy to fix any damned radio equipment he or the Navy had broken, but I warned him never ever to give me a list of Japanese radio frequencies and expect me to swim ashore alone again.

I was so upset that if he decided to kick me out of the Navy, well let it be!

Captain D—all the men called him that—ordered his yeoman out of the room and tried his best to calm me down. Captain D was certainly not afraid of me. I stood 5 feet, 7 1/2-inches in my stocking feet. I only weighed 128 pounds when I first enlisted. But after several years of regular Navy chow, by the time I earned my honorable discharge after the war ended, I weighed 140 pounds.

Captain D, on the other hand, was a large-boned man. He stood about 6-feet and, as far as I could tell, he was solid muscle. His hair was coal black, but he always wore it cut very short. Although his haircut was regulation Navy, that was the only thing about Captain D that could be considered military. His mission and his men came first.

Most likely it was not easy being in charge of the U.S. Navy's communications branch during the Allied force's march back through the Pacific islands. All of us, partly by nature but mostly due to extreme conditions of our infiltration duties, were rebels. We all wore our hair longer than most of the other servicemen. And we usually only wore parts of the issued uniform, whatever that happened to be. For example, I hated the sleeves on my combat fatigues. One of the first things I did whenever I landed on an island and before changing into my combat uniform was to cut off the shirt sleeves with my K-bar knife.

One other difference between the radio jammers and Captain D, I don't remember ever seeing him smoke even though the rest of us lit up as regularly as a blast furnace. I smoked off and on throughout my Navy career. But whenever I went ashore on my special operations missions, I quit smoking for several weeks prior to infiltration. I did not want the distraction. On those occasions, my job was to be as inconspicuous as possible.

Since my father had sold tobacco and alcohol and quit using either one, I always believed that I could use them both until I had enough, then just say no as my father had done. I smoked off and on clear through the time I was in college following the war. But after the war ended, nightmares and daytime memories of what I had done caused me to smoke quite a lot more than usual. Even then, however, I always knew that I could quit!

After Captain D had calmed me down, he generously offered me the use of a jeep. He then very calmly but firmly suggested that I was to pack up all of my spear fishing gear, haul it out to the windward side of Oahu, and enjoy some quiet time just camping, snorkeling and spearing tropical fish.

I wondered at the time how Captain D knew what I did in my spare time. And who had told him that I enjoyed spear fishing on the windward side of the island on my rare days off!

Years later, while reminiscing with a former grade school friend with whom I had later also shared a room in college, I learned that because

I'll Never Go Again! 31

my security classification during the war was so high, people all around me were ordered to make notes every half-hour as to my exact location and activity. My old friend said he knew these things because he had served in the U.S. Air Corps and it was his job during the war to type up any activity reports on men like me.

Following my brief time of rest and relaxation spent spear fishing on the opposite side of Oahu from Pearl harbor, the surviving eight men in our amphibious landing group were ordered to turn out on the parade field in our dress uniforms. There, we were told to wait at attention. An officer finally came along and handed out combat stars and ribbons to those of us who had invaded Guam. When the officer came to a halt in front of me he paused, looked at me and my rank, then said:

"You were lucky, Sparks. I didn't expect you to come baaaaaack!"

"Lucky" became my nickname for the rest of the war. All radio technicians and operators were commonly referred to as Sparks because of the insignia we all wore on our uniforms to indicate training and rank.

Returning home following the war, at first I never told anyone about my "Lucky" nickname. Due primarily to guilt and remorse, I was reluctant to explain the significance of that officer's pronouncement. During World War II, however, so many times the other Special Operations guys would joke around with me. My wartime buddies just loved to exaggerate and drawl out the last word as they repeated that commander's final line:

"I didn't expect you to come BAAAAAAAAaaaaack!"

Among those in my unit who did make it back alive after the first few invasions, one man started drinking hot sauce right from the bottle in an attempt to ruin his stomach. That way, he figured he would have a medical excuse not to go ashore ever again on an enemy-held island.

Another man in our unit went to sick bay every day where he would complain long and hard about the pain in his back. It seems he fell while doing some pre-invasion reconnaissance and somehow injured his back.

I didn't want to go on another of those missions ever again either, especially five whole days before a U.S. invasion force landed. But a most disastrous thing happened to me once I returned from my spear-fishing trip. While gambling with some of the other sailors, one guy who had survived the assault on Guadalcanal listened to all our complaints. Finally, he said this:

"Lucky, you realize that if you don't go the next time, the Navy will just have to send in some young kid who has never faced the lion and then that man will have to go!"

It was so shocking. I never could get over that statement! I can still hear him say it to me today! To "face the lion" meant that someone had engaged the enemy in hand-to-hand combat, either with guns or knives, and survived to tell about it. That was our phrase for those who had gone ashore when the Japanese soldiers still had sole possession of an island.

I was so mad at that guy! Because of him, I knew right then and there that I could not quit. I could not allow some kid who had never faced the lion to go ashore in my stead.

Although I never expected to live through any of the seven landings for which I eventually volunteered, I continued to swim ashore whenever they asked me to because I never wanted to be responsible for sending someone else. Each time, Captain D would say to me, "You'll come back. And you will go to college after the war!"

I was certainly not a Christian at that time. I was just an atheist human.

After the war was over, I went to some American Legion meetings. But I eventually stopped attending because they upset me so badly. I would listen to the other veterans talk about their bravery and how they were never afraid. That is usually the time of the meeting when I would stand up and call them all liars.

"We were all scared!" I said. "And we were all sure that we would never live through another landing."

CHAPTER SIX

"IF I DON'T COME BACK..."

Whenever our unit was getting ready for an amphibious assault, the other guys and I would sit around a poker table. We would deal the cards, drink beers or liquor if we had any, and play a game we called "If I don't come back." In the game, each of us would take turns saying, "If I don't come back, one of you guys will have to...."

To conclude that statement, each of us had our own special ending. When it was my turn, I always said, "One of you will have to break the bank (hit a large jackpot) at a casino in Reno and say, 'This is for Lucky.'"

There was a kid in our unit named Sullivan who had grown up on a farm somewhere in Colorado. He would always say, "One of you has to be a farmer and say then that, 'This is for Sullivan.'"

I remember another amphibious assault sailor by the name of John who would always say, "One of you will have to save your money for a month and then take out a gorgeous gal with long blonde hair. You'll have the biggest weekend of your life. And at the end of that weekend, you will say to her, 'This was for John.'"

There were many similar instructions about saving up for a date, or wearing certain clothes while going out on the town. For example, one sailor always said:

"You have to wear a tweed suit when you take my gal out."

Whenever the game of "If I don't make it back" was making its usual rounds, I would take out my "lucky" pair of dice and instigate a craps game. The lucky pair of dice I had were called tops and bottoms—that is dice with which you could never roll a seven. The same number was marked on the top of each dice as on the bottom. The pair were the same red color as a regular set of dice, and all I had to do was distract the other players for just one second as I slipped them out of my pocket and into a game.

Then, after I had taken all of the other players for some of their money, I would distract them all again and put the regular dice back into play before I turned them loose.

On that particular occasion, when I used the tops and bottoms, I just about cleaned all of the other guys out of every last penny. That is when we finally stopped shooting craps and started yet another round of "If I don't come back." This time, however, there was an especially long silence.

I believe we were all thinking that there was a very real possibility that none of us would come back alive from the next invasion. Just at the point when the silence started to become unbearable, one of my fellow radio operators—a guy by the nickname of "Socks" Rodgers spoke up. Socks was one of those guys who didn't participate in any of our gambling or carousing. Socks never so much as went out with us when we were on leave. He never got drunk and never was in trouble. Instead, he would usually just sit quietly on his bunk and read a religious book. Standing at about 5-foot, 10-inches, Socks was nearly three inches taller than me. He rarely ever joined any of our discussions. But when he did talk with any of us, he had a strange habit of cocking his head to one side. I believe he did that because he was so self-conscious.

Despite all of that, though, Socks was the best radio operator that I ever saw in the entire amphibious assault unit. That guy could read radio signals through enemy frequency jamming better than any other radio operator I have ever had the pleasure to meet.

On this occasion, Socks actually addressed the rest of us as he sat on his nearby bunk.

"If I Don't Come Back…"

"If I don't come back…," Socks finally said to break the long silence, "One of you will have to go to church at least once for me and say, 'I did this for Socks.'"

We were all shocked and silent for quite a while after that.

Socks got his nickname after he went ashore during the invasion of Guadalcanal. He was not able to change his socks for a few days during the invasion. As a result, he ended up with a bad case of jungle rot—ulcers caused by skin disease. A particularly virulent foot fungus had taken up residence on the bottoms of both feet and between his toes. His feet never really cleared up completely. For many months following Guadalcanal, whenever Socks heard gunfire he would react by taking off his shoes, pouring water into his upside-down helmet, and washing out his socks.

That's how he got his nickname. He was always washing his socks. You see, in our line of pre-invasion work during the war, there was bound to be a whole lot of gunfire. Socks survived all of the Pacific island invasions until we landed on Okinawa where he was killed.

For my part, I never really expected to live through the war. Of the 200 guys in my amphibious commando unit, only two of us survived. But when the war finally ended and I was still alive, I thought back on the many rounds of "If I don't come back" game we all had played.

I concluded then and there that since I'm not much of a lady's man, I couldn't really fulfill John's charge for a date with a beautiful blonde. Furthermore, since I could never survive as a farmer, Sullivan's wish would never suit me either.

Another sailor I met while I was at the Navy's discharge base wanted to partner up with someone and take up some homestead land near Tule Lake. The homesteads were only available for veterans. He said that we could become successful farmers, then turn around and sell the land for big money. I doubted that he and I could ever succeed at that. Working on a ranch for a short time had already convinced me that I hated every part of working the land.

Similarly, I went through each of the other guys' wishes and eliminated them all. None of them really seemed to fit me.

Certainly, I could never take Sock's place at church, could I?

CHAPTER SEVEN
THE CHURCH

Thinking about the challenge that Socks had laid on my soul brought back a flood of boyhood memories about the only church I knew at the time.

Directly across the street from a saloon that my mother operated in Portland, Oregon, stood a small church. Only a service station on a small point of land really separated the two buildings. As a young boy, it seemed to me they were on opposite sides of the world from each other. My entire family would go to the bar on Sunday mornings to clean up the place after a busy Saturday night. We had to be ready to open the saloon at noon on Sundays. I would stand behind the bar and look across the street right at the front doors of that church.

Every Sunday noon, without fail, there would be three "regulars" who came out the door of that church and walked straight to our saloon. They sat on the same stools every single time, hence the name regulars. But other than those three crossovers, we had little other contact with folks from that church. At school, I knew a few older kids who attended the church, but they would regularly trip me, push me down and kick me. They jeered and called my mother a barmaid or worse whenever they saw me walking home from school.

I connected their meanness with the church. As I got older, whenever anyone grabbed me by the shirt and told me that I needed to be saved, I just kicked them badly until they turned me loose.

'Why don't we go to church?" I once asked my stepfather Sarge one Sunday morning while we were cleaning up the saloon.

"When your left and right fists can't take care of you, then you go (to church) so you'll have others to help you fight," was Sarge's reply.

I assumed from his statement that churchgoers were a gang that ran together and that they would naturally fight any intruders. My family knew all about gangs. My parents were operating their saloon on the fringe of the law. It was legal in those days to have a beer joint, but they quickly put up a partition across the room and operated a speakeasy, an illegal hard liquor and gambling joint, in the back. The mob or syndicate made regular payoffs to the police and that is what kept our family's saloon from getting busted.

Once I even asked Lew Stringham, head of the syndicate in Portland, if he went to church. He would frequent my parent's saloon whenever he was in Portland, Ore.

"No! I don't give money to no one. I'm an atheist!" he said to me. Stringham explained that if you went to a church, you were expected to give 10 percent of all you earned to that church.

Since I didn't give any money to anyone either, I was convinced that I, too, was an atheist.

Listening to all of the guys saying their "If I don't come backs" began to bother me. I wondered how I was ever going to fulfill one of their requests if I made it through the war alive. Likewise, I also thought a lot about Captain D and what he always said to me before each mission. Captain D would say:

"Lucky, you'll make it back. And after the war, you will go to college!"

Captain D stunned me. No one in my family had ever gone to college!

It wasn't much time at all before I was given another long list of Japanese radio frequencies to memorize, along with another map of hills on some island. All told, during my time of seeing action in World

The Church

War II, I landed on seven different enemy held islands. Not all of the landings, however, involved my swimming ashore. At Iwo Jima the beaches and hills were so lacking in vegetation that I wondered several times during the invasion where I would hide.

CHAPTER EIGHT
THE WAR CONTINUES

I swam ashore on three islands that only had numbers, no names, as far as I can remember. They were part of a long chain of observation outposts established by the Japanese to keep an eye on allied naval and air operations throughout the Pacific. I understood that the Japanese soldiers on these island outposts would watch the U.S. ships go by and identify them if they could. They then relayed the information to Japan or a nearby Japanese naval unit. The soldiers on these coral atolls had really good camouflage.

I was included in the pre-invasion operations on these atolls because my superiors wanted me to extract the oscillators out of the enemy's big radio transmitting equipment before our troops destroyed the remaining enemy communications equipment with explosives. The U.S. War Department analysts wanted to see what changes the enemy was making in their radio transmission equipment.

On the first two islands, allied forces encountered minimal resistance. We lost only two or three of our own men. So when the third atoll invasion came, we landed and weren't too surprised when there was absolutely no resistance at all.

I and several other soldiers went to the hilltop where one of the Japanese radio transmitters was well camouflaged. We didn't see any Japanese soldiers there either, so we began scouting operations throughout a little valley almost to the other side of the island. Finally, a few of our scouts came back moving very quickly and told the "Old Man," our Skipper, that the last of the Japanese soldiers were leaving the island on the other side by climbing aboard some small boats.

I was up at the front end of the patrol column when I heard one of the marines nearby commenting on the scouting report. He said, "If we don't fire a shot, we won't get a battle star."

It wasn't a minute later when that same marine opened fire into the jungle just to my right side. We all hit the ground because at the same time he hollered, "Sniper in that tree!"

I believe I heard at least a hundred rounds fired before the Old Man finally called a halt to the shooting and sent a few scouts out to reconnoiter. They eventually reported back that the sniper apparently had slipped away. Years afterwards, when I was able to attend the marine boot camp graduation ceremony of a grandson-in-law, I visited the U.S. Marine museum. The guide was a World War II veteran, and when he saw me with tears running down my face, he asked me if I was a Marine in the "Big One?"

"No." I responded. "I was a member of the U.S. Navy Amphibious Assault or Special Forces."

I then told him the story of that fake battle and he almost choked. He said, "If you tell that story around here again, they will certainly hang you!"

That is just one of the things I could tell that they likely don't want to hear.

In the beginning of my Special Forces training, I was determined not to do any more killing than was absolutely required. But there was a scout in one Marine division who was a big Indian. He told us once that when his father died, he would become chief of his tribe back home. So, we called him "Chief."

Despite his large size, Chief could slip out as a scout and come back with some of the best information of any of us. He usually searched the bodies of the Japanese soldiers that he killed and took out with him all of their letters from home and family photographs. From this I learned

The War Continues

the Japanese soldiers were no different from us in terms of carrying keepsake memories with them.

Chief always had quite a few pieces of this wartime plunder on his person. I shared with him that my grandmother was an Oglalla Sioux, and that is how we became close friends. Chief was big. He stood well over six feet, and probably weighed 200 pounds dripping wet. He was the closest thing I had to a friend during World War II. He was heavily muscled. One of Chief's favorite pastimes was to run the obstacle course. The rest of the guys would all be drinking, talking or gambling, and there Chief would be outside, in all types of weather, running the obstacle course.

Cutline information: July 1944. Two views of the same church in the Philippines where Japanese soldiers were hiding. The left view was taking during an actual assault. The right view was taken after the war ended.

From a Speakeasy to the Cross

Following every pre-invasion swim ashore after Guam, the Navy would evacuate the amphibious men to a small, uninhabited island where all of us could decompress. The officers always made sure there was a bar set up where we could each get two free beers at a time. They also supplied the beach area with a Military Police patrol to keep those who drank too much from falling into the water and drowning.

If you wanted more than two beers, you had to go through the line again or ask someone else to go through for you. I am the type of person who does not like to lose self-control. I discovered this as a teenager: When I drank recklessly I would black out. My father was an alcoholic, so I guess I inherited some of his traits. Because I did not want to lose control of myself, I usually went through the beer line only once for myself.

Chief knew this, and often he would have me go through the line for him. After one particular mission, we had done this. But Chief had a particularly rough time of things on his scouting mission and he told me he wanted more beer. We then asked two other guys to go through the line for each of us. That gave Chief a total of eight beers in a very short time period.

As we drank our beer, Chief and I started talking about Indian ways. We were walking on the beach and we gradually got out of bounds, far away from the beach patrols. By this time, Chief was well into a gigantic drunk. He finally passed out from the alcohol. Well, he was a big man and I wasn't. But I knew I had to get him back to the authorized area without getting either of us in trouble. I ended up dragging him through the surf. I held onto one of Chief's hands while with my other hand I grabbed his hair to keep his mouth and nose out of the water. That is how I floated him back to our authorized drinking area. The Military Police pulled Chief out of the surf and demanded to know how the two of us had managed to get beyond the limits. Apparently they were busy with another man when we walked down the beach, I told them.

We usually operated alone, but on our only landing together, Chief and I swam ashore side by side in the Philippines. Later, Chief went out on patrol as a scout with his usual collection of battle souvenirs stuffed into a shirt pocket. When he did not come back in a reasonable amount of time, the commanding officer sent another patrol out after him to see

The War Continues 45

if Chief had somehow been wounded. I went along to operate the special radio equipment we carried. It was new equipment and the Japanese could not jam it very easily.

All of a sudden, the scouts reported back to our patrol unit. They were looking pretty grim. Eventually, they took us to a location where Japanese soldiers had apparently bent over and tied two trees to the ground. The Japanese had then tied Chief's arms and legs to the bent over tree trunks. When they cut the ropes holding the two trees down, the trees sprang upright again, literally tearing Chief's body into pieces.

Our guess was that Chief's death had been slow and painful because of the many ropes tied at different heights along both tree trunks. Chief's usual collection of Japanese soldiers' pictures and letters from home were also missing.

That encounter changed me!

A few of the U.S. Marines we worked with had already started to castrate Japanese soldiers whenever they caught them alive. Those of us who were the first ashore did not take any prisoners. After all, what would we do with them?

But these early wave troops who could not take live prisoners began to dry the testicles of the castrated Japanese prisoners. A few even made necklaces out of the dried testicles and wore them to show off how many of the enemy they had captured. According to the rules as I heard them from the Marines, you could only take one testicle for a necklace. And it had to be taken from a live prisoner.

The first enemy soldier that I killed other than those I encountered on beach patrol was a young Japanese soldier who surprised me as I was going to one of the many island hills to jam their communications equipment. He surprised me with a command in Japanese that I did not understand. I turned around and instantly remembered one of the things I had been taught by a bar fighter while I was still a kid.

I raised both of my hands and began to shake like a leaf. The enemy soldier continued to give me orders in Japanese. I did not understand. I just played scared and shook. He came towards me with his rifle and bayonet kind of pointed up into the air. I sensed he was going to shove me to the ground.

When he drew close enough to me, I kicked him on the leg, just under the kneecap in the same way I had learned in a saloon fight not too many years before. The Japanese soldier couldn't even fire his weapon because the force of my kick had hurt him so badly that he just crumpled to the ground.

I killed him for Chief. And then I started my own necklace!

The guy in the bar who had taught me to kick like that was about my same height—about 5-feet, 7-inches. But look out! That kick move can really mess up those who challenge you.

I soon heard the rest of the Japanese patrol unit closing in, so I once again went into the nature position and became as still as a stump or a log. When I came out of the meditative state some time afterwards, I waited for a long time before I moved. Even then, I took only a few slow, quiet steps. The remaining Japanese soldiers were long gone, so I continued on to the next hilltop to knock out more of their radio equipment. This same sort of action repeated itself countless times from my first landing on Guam to my final landing on Okinawa.

Many times I went "banana hunting" with marines. That is what we called hunting for Japanese soldiers who had somehow become separated from their own units or bunch. Since we often were among the first ones ashore, we were instructed time and again never to take any prisoners.

That command was countered only once that I can recall. It was while I was stationed on Okinawa to repair one of our own radio transmitters in the relative comfort of a command tent. I overheard a Captain tell two officers whom he had called in for a report that on their next patrol they were to bring back prisoners.

Then he said to each of them,

"Repeat the order for me: You will bring back prisoners."

They each replied, "We are to bring back prisoners! Sir."

It just so happened that I went out with that same patrol unit to carry some high frequency radio equipment that was considered top secret and classified. We brought back prisoners. It was on that same patrol that we saw Japanese soldiers ransacking a native village. Through our field glasses, we could seem them raping the native women. We slipped

The War Continues 47

in to the village after them and brought back two prisoners. The rest, we killed and castrated.

During the past sixty years since the war ended, I have often felt guilt and shame because of the necklace incident. But the killing of Chief had been equally brutal and terrible. It wasn't until 2004, when my doctor urged me to read a book titled "Fly Boys" that I was finally able to let go of some of my guilty feelings.

CHAPTER NINE
THE PERSIAN GULF

When the peace treaty with the Japanese was finally signed, I went ashore with the first wave for the purpose of having communications with the SOPA (senior officer present afloat.) This initial landing turned into a project to build a radio station broadcasting to the occupying U.S. troops. It surprised me to have Japanese men bow to me as I approached. They sure knew how to accept defeat, I thought.

By this time in the war, I had earned enough points to go home and be discharged because of the type and length of my service. But the base officers told me that if I pressed for a discharge, then the Navy brass would have me declared essential. That way, I wouldn't be allowed to leave. It wasn't too long after I learned that when they woke me up about 4 A.M. and had me hurriedly pack all of my things. They ordered me to report to a particular building. I thought this meant I was finally going home. When I got to the building, they ordered us to strip down. Then they wrote uniform size numbers right on our skin. For example, 28 for the waist, 9 for the shoes, etc. The real surprise was that we were being measured for new combat gear. But it was desert camouflage this time.

I still thought all of this had something to do with my discharge. I guessed that I had to be outfitted properly before I was allowed to go home. At the very end of a long line, the procurement petty officer told me to sign for a new rifle. I refused! Without saying a word, the man simply turned his receipt book around and wrote in my name. Once outfitted, our orders were to dress in the new uniform. Then, we were ordered to report to a different building for bunk assignments.

I smelled a rat!

I did not get dressed. I simply walked naked out of the building into a light rain dragging my new uniform and other clothes in a mattress cover. I was also dragging the butt of my new rifle along the ground by simply holding onto its barrel.

Suddenly, a booming voice behind me yelled: "ATTENTION!"

I stood erect as a Marine Corps officer with gold on his hat approached me.

"Where do you think you are going, Sailor?" the full bird colonel asked.

I replied with the building number we were supposed to report to. The colonel looked so shocked I thought he was going to die.

He said he was the commanding officer in charge of a super secret operation in the Persian Gulf. He informed me that I would be part of this operation. He then ordered me to get to the barracks pronto and be ready for inspection within 30 minutes.

"Yes, sir!" I responded, then ran to the building.

A lot of my clothes were wet from having being dragged through the rain. Some of the other men loaned me articles of dry clothing to wear. By the time the colonel arrived, my clothes were all properly rolled and ready for inspection. But that didn't stop him from asking what was my problem.

"Nothing, sir," I replied.

From that time on, the colonel never spoke to me except to give a direct order.

It seems that an outcast son of the ruling sheik of Saudi Arabia had put together a cavalry unit with help from the Russians to take over the oil fields along the Persian Gulf. These were the same oil wells from which oil was piped to the port city of R'as Tanurah, just north of Bahrain. We went ashore from a U.S. Navy tanker transport vessel just as if we were landing on yet another island in the Pacific. We set up

The Persian Gulf 51

sand bags, machine gun nests and everything we needed to secure the oil fields. Some time after we landed, the Arab cavalry showed up. They were armed with long barreled rifles like those used in the Old West. Meanwhile, we were equipped with the very latest issue of weaponry available in the mid-1940s. It was not even a fair contest!

Our commander ordered our machine gunners to spray the sand in front of the Arab cavalry, which they did. Once the smoke and dust cleared, we looked up but there was not a single Arab horseman remaining anywhere in sight. They had disappeared as completely as if they had melted into the sand. They never were to be seen again. The oil field was later to become part of the Oil & Petroleum Exporting Countries (O.P.E.C.) but at that time, the British government controlled it.

Following this brief skirmish, we headed back to Hawaii.

A thick fog was covering nearly the entire Persian Gulf, however, so we were running the tanker transporter by directional transmitters and radar. Suddenly, our ship hit a rock that apparently had been previously struck by many other ships. The rumor going around was that someone—most probably the Russians—had moved one of our key directional transmitters about a mile from where it should have been located.

That really confused us. But luckily we were able to gun the ships engines enough to back off of the rock. We ended up grounding our tanker ship on a nearby sandy beach instead. Some of the oil we had taken aboard the tanker was leaking out but at least we were safe. They salvaged the oil that remained by pumping it to undamaged tanks on the other end of the tanker.

That transfer of weight also made the ship rise considerably in the nose. When the hole that had been ripped in the hull by the rocks finally rose enough above the water's surface, we shoved mattresses and cargo netting in to close up the hole.

Meanwhile, the U.S. Navy sent a repair ship that poured a layer of concrete between the metal hull of the ship and the mattresses. They re-loaded the tanker with oil to replace what had leaked out, and off we headed back to Guam for repairs.

But when we finally reached Guam nearly a week later, the shipyard there was so full of vessels damaged in the recently completed war with

Japan that the ship was ordered to sail another 3,300 miles further east to Pearl Harbor in Hawaii.

While we waited at Pearl Harbor for our discharge orders, the Navy housed us in temporary quarters at the now-unused Base Hospital 39. It was during that period that Captain D, who was like a father to me, encouraged me to apply for a college extension course. Congress had just passed the GI Bill, which helped a lot of guys who served in the war start college once they got out. First exposed to higher education during boot camp while taking some radio technician classes at Wright College in Chicago, I was eager to get started. With Captain D's help, I applied for a scholarship number and started taking college classes until my honorable discharge could be properly processed.

CHAPTER TEN

SPEAKEASIES

No one in my family had ever attended college before me. In fact, I was fortunate to have made it through two years of high school. Seizures plagued me for years as a young boy. Back in those days, if a child had seizures of any kind, the school authorities would not let the parents enroll the child in school unless the child had been free of seizures for at least a year.

Years later, when my middle child Charlotte was still an infant she suffered from the same problem. My wife and I took her to a specialist in San Francisco who diagnosed a form of epilepsy, which my daughter thankfully outgrew. The specialist needed a complete family history, and so he took a look at the records my mother had kept of the frequency and duration of my own seizures. After a brief review, the specialist told me that I was lucky to be as tall as I was as the seizures I suffered as a child can often halt the production of growth hormones.

As a young boy, it was a painful experience every year for me to watch the other kids start school. One year I was really looking forward to starting school, but as I sat in a barber's chair getting the customary cut just before classes started, I had a convulsion. There went another year!

From a Speakeasy to the Cross

Neither my mother nor I would have told anyone, but unfortunately, we lived in a small town. A teacher lived right across the street from us and she told the school authorities. When I finally was able to attend school, my mother simply bought a revised birth certificate from the syndicate indicating I was the correct age for starting first grade.

All other records of my birth date were then destroyed. In the speakeasies, we sold birth, death and marriage certificates. The syndicate's hoodlums had the necessary contacts to make sure the falsified records were the only ones that existed.

The syndicate would look for a clerk who wrote up entries in the official books for a city, county or state. Entries were all hand written in those days and the record pages simply were bolted together. Bolts can be removed, however, and new pages written. All the syndicate had to do was help the clerk get a relative out of court, jail or some other trouble. Once the clerk had falsified the official books even once, they were in danger of losing their jobs or going to jail if discovered. Using threats of blackmail, the syndicate forced them to continue falsifying other records whenever requested.

I grew up with a first hand knowledge of speakeasies—sometimes we shortened it to 'speak' in those days—and the payoffs to officers of the law and courts. My father, Arthur, owned several businesses that were considered illegal at the time. He was a route salesman who sold beer, tobacco and candy. That was the legal part of his business. Prohibition had ended in 1933. But for several years after, up until he died in 1937, my father would also peddle bootleg whiskey out of a hidden compartment in his truck.

He made nothing but money. We lived in the best part of Vancouver, and my father was a Grand Master in the Masonic Lodge. Every other year, my father would buy a brand new car. My mom, Birdie, was half Indian. She always operated the saloon when my dad was making his sales rounds. At the back of the saloon, we had a speakeasy.

Speakeasies were hard liquor drinking and gambling establishments that became popular during prohibition. At that time, both activities were against the law. Usually, they were operated in conjunction with a legitimate business. In the case of my parents' speakeasy, patrons had to give a secret password to get in. We had a large bolt on the inside of

Speakeasies

the door, but it was mostly just for show. We didn't really need to bolt it to keep the cops out because we always paid them off.

The reason they were called speakeasies is because patrons were always supposed to speak in a low voice since the operation was not legal.

The police would stage phony raids on the speakeasies whenever local political pressure demanded that some action be taken on the illegal drinking and gambling establishments around town. This was usually sparked by some politician trying to get the conservative vote. The cops would always tell us ahead of time when the raids were going to happen. We would inform our customers that they may not want to be at our place on such and such a date.

The police always made a big show of arresting a few people. Well, some of our regular patrons thought it was exciting. They would show up and want to be arrested in the phony raids. They knew that nothing serious would happen to them. They were usually hauled down to the station house downtown, and let off with a simple warning.

As a result, I just had no respect for law and government. When my father died in 1937, we liquidated everything to pay his medical bills. All that remained was $50 a month from his life insurance, and our home. My father was convinced that we would live well on $50 a month because it was the middle of the depression. After my father died, we sold our house in Vancouver, and bought a "Beer Joint" in Portland.

We immediately converted it into an illegal operation—known in the syndicate as a "doughnut" business. In one front corner we had a small bar where beer was served. This was all legal in 1937.

But we converted the saloon's much larger back room into a wide-open liquor bar and gambling operation. Our connection to organized crime was called by many names. We called it "The Syndicate," but at times my family also said "Mafiosi."

One day, as I was walking through the alley behind our saloon, I saw my mother standing at the back door. She was counting out a stack of twenty-dollar bills into the hands of a sheriff's deputy.

We knew the deputy and even called him "Whitey" because of his blond hair. After Mom gave him the money, he wrote her a receipt. I approached him as he was climbing back into his patrol car,

"You are probably the richest guy in town, Whitey," I observed.

"If you think I get to keep any of this you are crazy!" he responded. "It all goes to the Sheriff, the Police Chief and the Judges," Whitey explained.

The syndicate even launched me in a small business as a child. Before each Fourth of July, I would set up a fireworks stand. The syndicate supplied the fireworks that I sold. Any money I made was used to buy me school clothes. There were several other kids with fireworks stands in town.

Around town, it was common knowledge that if anyone brought any fireworks in from out of state and tried to compete with the syndicate's own stands, their small booths and inventory would soon go up in a ball of flames. The police never investigated any of these suspicious fires, as far as I ever knew.

CHAPTER ELEVEN
THE NEIGHBORHOOD

Since my mother went down to open the saloon by noon and came home only after the saloon had closed—usually not until 3 A.M.—I always got myself up, dressed and fixed my own breakfast every day.

As I got older, I began to hang out with a bunch of kids that were as free as I was to go out at night. We would drink beer and eventually began getting into fights with kids from other neighborhoods.

If the police came to break it up, they would line us up, usually with our backs to the wall. The police would then ask if our folks had a phone and what were their names?

All I answered was that my father was Lew Stringham, who headed up the syndicate in Portland. Of course I was lying since my father had died, but I said it to protect myself. Whenever I told them that, the police would immediately ask me if I had bus fare home. They would just let me go without so much as a lecture.

One day, talk at the saloon was that the people had voted in a new mayor and other officials. I didn't pay much attention to it then, but later, when we kids got in another fight downtown, the law came and broke it up.

The police asked their usual questions. I again told them my father was Lew Stringham.

This time, however, they had me turn around and they put handcuffs on me.

"You'll be in trouble for this," I brazenly told the police.

The officer's reply was something to the effect that at last he got to be a cop.

When they telephoned my parents that time, my stepfather Sarge came down to the police station to get me. He managed to give me hell all the way home.

Sometime later, word around town was that the syndicate had once again regained control of the police. After an election all it usually took was for the syndicate to help someone illegally or buy them off. If these methods didn't work, there was always the threat of harming a person's family members.

For years after we all had moved away from Oregon, my brother and his wife saved newspaper clippings of people who reportedly had acid thrown in their face. It didn't make any difference if the suspect was a nut or not. Who would know whether the mob had hired it done. The mob kept both the population and politicians under their control more by helping them or threatening them than actually harming them, but we were still afraid of what they might do to us or the ones we loved.

CHAPTER TWELVE

THE FOUNTAIN FAMILY

At my house there was a rule that if I was leaving town for a day or more I had to write a note and leave it on the kitchen table for my mother.

One of the years just before World War II broke out, and a day or two following the fourth of July, I left such a note and took a bus down to San Francisco for a visit with my aunt and uncle. My brother also lived nearby, across the bay, but he worked every day. My aunt and uncle were each in their seventies and very quickly I determined they were boring to be with for a young man such as myself who was always seeking adventure. Shortly after I arrived, I left a similar note on their kitchen table and just took off. I carried all of my clothes in a back pack that I had made from an old pair of blue jeans, a trick I learned while still in Boy Scouts up in Portland.

With nowhere in particular to go, I wandered around Golden Gate Park for a while. Hunger set in after a few hours until I saw a polo match going on. Figuring to find dropped coins lost by people seated in the bleachers, I went around under the seats looking for loose change. It was there that I ran into another kid who was apparently doing the same thing.

We got to talking and he finally asked me, "Where do you live?"

I responded vaguely that my father was dead and I hadn't seen my mother for a long time. Both statements were the truth, just not all of the truth.

"You should join with us at the fountain," he told me.

He next wanted to know whether I could read. Even though I assured him that I could, he walked me into the downtown area where he produced a third grade textbook and asked me to prove my education. He told me that if I couldn't read it, then I could go to a school out in Butcher Town, one of the nearby neighborhoods famous for its meat markets. Apparently there was a teacher who allowed members of the Fountain Family, as he described what I took to be a loose-knit group of street urchins, into a classroom so they could at least learn the essentials of reading and arithmetic.

In further discussions with my new friend, I learned that the Fountain Family was actually a very organized group of children who essentially lived on the streets of San Francisco until they turned 16. At that age, a former member of the Fountain Family would assist them in getting a job and starting out in a life of their own.

For the next several months, I was a full-fledged member of the Fountain Family. We would gather twice a day—in the morning and the evening—at the fountain where Market and Leavenworth streets meet. At the start of each meeting, the leader would take a head count to see if everyone was OK. Then, he would ask questions to determine whether each of us had enough money to buy food. We were never allowed to steal anything. We lived together only to keep from going to an orphanage where the authorities would not keep you virtually imprisoned until you turned 18.

There were about 15 of us youngsters in the Fountain Family when I joined. We all learned some very strict rules. The penalty for not obeying the rules was to get kicked out of the Fountain Family. During the period of time that I was a member, a young man whose mother worked as a prostitute kicked him out of her residence because she didn't want him around at night while she was working. She would rather he live on the street. He joined us at the fountain. I believe that the Fountain

The Fountain Family

Family graduates would donate funds on a regular basis to the group's leader so no one in the group would ever be allowed to go hungry or resort to stealing.

If a homosexual—we called them queers in those days—bothered us, the Fountain Family graduates would form a posse and take him out to the beach where he was beaten so badly that he would never bother any of us ever again. That was street justice.

After living on the street with that gang for several months, I rode the bus back to Portland. Without much in the way of explanation for my long absence, I returned to classes at Benson High School, a technical school, where I was training for work in a radio station. That was my second year of high school, and my last!

Following the completion of school that year, I dropped out and went to work in one place after another. I had worked part-time and summers ever since completing the sixth grade. If I had a job application that required my mother to sign it, I could put down any age I wanted or needed to be to get the job. We were never allowed to talk about my birthday or the birth certificate I had been given by the syndicate. Since it came from the syndicate, we couldn't tell anyone that they sold those types of certificates or our family would be punished severely.

I was in my sixties when my wife and I once returned to San Francisco to visit my brother. Even after all those years, he would still usher me out onto the patio outside before he asked me about my birth date. He lived in mortal fear that members of the Syndicate would throw acid in his wife's face or cripple his children if we told anything.

CHAPTER THIRTEEN

YOU'RE IN THE NAVY NOW!

Growing up with first-hand knowledge of corruption in government, I just assumed my fate was to be a draft dodger when World War II started.

Registering for the draft with my real age was a real problem since I wasn't sure what year to put down for my birth. So, I decided to talk with Lew Stringham about the problem. Stringham came to my mother's saloon for lunch whenever he was in town. That is when I decided to talk to him. It was from those infrequent talks with Lew that I discovered how the Syndicate got the birth, death and marriage certificates that we sold, and how they were made legal.

"Don't worry!" Stringham told me when I brought up the military service question. "I'll get you a draft card when you need it."

By that time in my life, I was working for RCA at a most menial task. My job consisted of taping wires together so they would fit neatly into the machine cases.

Lew found out from my mother that I was studying in the library and was into college mathematics by the eighth grade. It was the arithmetic teacher who had sent me there and provided the books for me to go through and work every problem. This was so much better than listening to the other students asking dumb questions in class and my getting into trouble.

My friend Bob drank a lot with me nearly every night. One weekend, Bob got in trouble with his mother. He had moved out of the house and into a room over the garage that his parents often rented out for extra income. Wanting to test the limits of his newly-found independence, Bob had invited a girl over to see his new place.

Well, Bob's mother caught him with the girl in his room so she chased her own son with a butcher knife. I saw this happen because I was outside Bob's room just sitting in my parked car. When I first saw Bob's mother run to the kitchen for the knife, I also noticed that Bob's girl ran off naked down the street in the other direction.

As soon as it appeared that the garage apartment was vacant, I crept upstairs to Bob's room and rescued the girl's clothing. Then, I drove down about a block in the same direction that I had seen her running until I came to some hazelnut bushes. I figured she must be hiding there, so I called out to her. I waited and nothing much happened until I happened to mention that I had her clothes waiting in the car with me.

Like a shot she jumped into my car and dressed herself as fast as she could manage. She then told me her address so I could take her home. Afterwards, I went looking for Bob. When I found him, he decided it might be safer to come back to my house to stay for a time with me. During my growing up years, quite a few of my friends and acquaintances came home with me to stay for a night or two.

Most of them were too afraid to go home when they were drunk.

The Friday night after I rescued Bob and his girl, we got together again. We started drinking. That night, Bob argued with me. He said that we ought to enlist in the Navy.

I argued with him to no end. But still half drunk the next morning, Saturday, we both found our way to the Navy recruiting station downtown.

The recruiting officers gave each of us a series of tests and we filled out what seemed like endless pages of questions. At one point, the recruiter asked me what was my religious preference.

I told him that I was an atheist!

You're in the Navy Now!

He pondered that statement for a moment, then he told me that there was no "A" for atheist on a soldier's dog tags. He said he had a simple solution.

"Are you Jewish?" he said,

My reply was "You know I'm not!"

"Are you Catholic?" he then asked me.

Again I responded, "You know I'm not!"

Right then and there he made me Protestant because when I got to boot camp three days later, the U.S. Navy already had put a "P" for Protestant on my dog tags.

The recruiter also asked me about the technical high school I had attended. I explained earning two licenses. The first was a HAM operator's permit. The other was a Second Class commercial radio operator's license, which one needed if one was going to work in a radio station as I intended to do.

Next, the recruiter asked about the part of the enlistment form where I indicated earning a certificate as a Red Cross lifeguard. To verify that information, they gave me a written examination that they called the "Eddy Test." When I passed it, they told me that they would enlist me as a seaman first class and send me to radio technician's school immediately upon my successful completion of boot camp.

Of course, this didn't mean anything to me at the time. The recruiter gave Bob and I a date three days hence to report for the bus that would take us off to boot camp.

When we arrived at the recruiting station, we had been drinking and we were still in a silly mood. The recruiters must have been upset at us because Bob ended up being sent for basic training to Farragut, Idaho. Me they sent clear to the Great Lakes, a boot camp north of Chicago. I thought for years that they separated us just because we were drinking buddies.

It wasn't until many years later when discussing this with an old roommate who had served as a clerk in the Army Air Corps that he finally convinced me that the Navy knew exactly where I was bound shortly after my enlistment.

As it turned out, I attended boot camp for just four weeks while most other recruits had to attend for eight weeks. My whole company at boot camp only went four weeks before we all headed for special schools.

Unfortunately for me, I had so much freedom before joining the Navy that I was in trouble from the very beginning of boot camp.

One of the first things they subjected us to was a full physical examination. Then we received an entire series of vaccinations. My step-father Sarge had served in the U.S. Army for twenty-seven years. He was an infantry sergeant. His advice to me after he found out of my enlistment was to be sure to exercise immediately after any medical shots to avoid getting sick from them. Remembering his advice when receiving the shots, I headed straight to the gym.

There I found some young guys playing basketball on one end of the court. A colored guy was shooting baskets at the other end of the gym. I tried to get into the game with those white guys but they said the teams were even. They cut me off. So I decided to go down to the other end of the gym where I played one-on-one with the colored guy. The others finally all left to go down to the shower room and I was alone up there having a good time shooting baskets. When I finally grew tired of it, I went to the shower room and there were the other six white guys just waiting for me to show up.

They were southerners and they called me a "Nigger Lover." They told me they were going to teach me a lesson for playing basketball with a colored. I backed into a corner so they couldn't surround me, and I put up one helluva fight.

By the time it was all over, I know for a fact that I had kicked some groin and bit at least one ear. But I was down and beaten, so they finally left me alone with my bruises. The one thing I was sure of after the fight ended was that I knew what each of the other six guys looked like.

As the days wore on, I found the first one in the mess hall. I jumped him and gave him quite a beating before others in the room could get me off of him. For this infraction, I was sent to the brig, the name the Navy gives to a jail cell. Then I was called into a small room and lectured by an officer who warned me against fighting. Finally, I was dismissed and told to return to my unit. It was a couple of days before I spotted

You're in the Navy Now!

the second guy who had beaten me. I jumped him and he put up a bit of a fight for just a minute or two.

I kicked him in the face when he was down before anyone could stop me. Again, the military police took me to the brig.

When the disciplinary officer on duty called me in to talk, he apparently did not know anything about the previous fight with the other basketball player. He, too, gave me a lecture about fighting and told me that it simply was not allowed. I listened, but figured there were still four other basketball players to go before we were even.

I spotted the next one again in the mess hall. This time I was really angry. I jumped him but he did not even put up a fight. However, I was grabbed again by the Military Police and taken for a third time to the brig.

When I was called in before the duty officer, I'll never forget what he said.

"They are scraping the bottom of the barrel when they let men like you in the Navy." Then he asked me, "What's going on? This is the third time!"

I told him the whole story from the beginning. He told me that if I was to take revenge just once more, or get in any other type of trouble, then I would receive a bad conduct discharge!

I believe he meant it. I heard through the grapevine that all six of the basketball players who had jumped me were eventually ordered to report to the officer and each of them received a stern lecture and punishment. They each had to perform their regular duties as well as complete a straight week of mess hall duty in the evenings. They were also threatened as I had been with a dishonorable discharge.

I feared discharge so much that I tried very hard to behave myself. But it was difficult to adapt to this strange life in the military that placed so many limits on my personal freedom.

CHAPTER FOURTEEN
I NEED A VOLUNTEER

After just four weeks, I graduated from boot camp. But I did not get any leave time before sea duty as had all of the other sailors who attended boot camp in the regular classes. Instead, I was sent straight to Wright College in Chicago. There, I had four weeks of what they called intensive study. More than half of the students attending Wright College with me flunked out during that period of time. But I had gone through differential and integral calculus by the eighth grade studying by myself in the library. The college course work was no big deal for me.

After Wright College, the military brass had me skip another school experience. They chose instead to send me directly to Treasure Island in San Francisco Bay where I received the final stage of training for a radio technician's rating. At Treasure Island we were supposed to spend most of our time studying circuits. All the other students spent hours trying to memorize the three main types of radio-frequency wave oscillators: Colpitts, Hartley and Reflex.

I had already memorized them because I had to know them by heart in order to become a HAM operator. I have never been one to worry about trying to learn what I already knew. So I decided to spend my time at Treasure Island working in the various laboratories and becoming more familiar with the Navy's different types of radio receivers and transmitters. I was only there about two weeks when I got orders to report to the unit Captain's office.

"Sailor, I hear you do not study," he said to me.

My first thought was, 'What trouble am I in now?'

But I couldn't imagine that I could be in trouble for not studying!

Immediately I told the Captain that whenever the instructors gave me a test containing questions taken from a textbook, I could remember everything including the page numbers from where the questions came. Even though I do not actually have a photographic memory, that was the only excuse I could think of at the time in my own defense.

The Captain then commented, "According to your military records, you were an amateur radio operator?"

"Yes sir, I was a HAM," I replied.

Then he said, "It also says you are a Red Cross certified lifeguard."

"Yes, sir! And I worked at it," was my reply.

Finally, the Captain said to me, "Then it is obvious that you remember numbers really well."

Boy, howdy! Mathematics was my favorite subject in school and did I ever feel good until I suddenly recalled being in trouble for fighting while in boot camp. I was sure this was going to end up being yet another lecture complete with threats of dishonorable discharge.

But the Captain surprised me when he said, "Good, I need a volunteer. Take two steps forward!"

I took two steps forward even though I had no way of knowing what was about to happen next.

A short time later, a junior officer told me to forget my classes and just keep myself busy learning about the big transmitters and other radio equipment as I had already been doing. The junior officer indicated to me that it might take a few days until the Navy could issue me a new security clearance. Those "few days" eventually stretched into weeks. It wasn't until after the war was over that I learned the military authorities really came down hard on my mother and stepfather Sarge during that period. My mom told me it was a terrible experience.

During that period of time, the investigators informed me that my oldest brother was not my father's son. Apparently my mother had been

I Need a Volunteer

married before but her first husband died in an epidemic while she was still carrying his unborn baby. When she married my father, my parents just changed my brother's last name to Baker.

The investigators also wanted to know all about the illegal connections they thought I had with the syndicate. I told them that I had never been employed by the Mafia. I didn't consider working the fireworks stand as a boy to be employment.

They asked my step-father Sarge and me if he ever had contact with his family in Germany. He was born in Germany, but he had shipped out at a young age as a cabin boy and had never gone back.

I didn't know whether he had maintained contact with his German relatives, but I told them I seriously doubted it.

Apparently, they really worked Sarge over good.

There were also a lot of questions about the saloon my mother owned and whether its status as a business was legal.

"I just don't know," I told the investigators when they asked me these same questions.

Finally, the military investigators left me alone and an officer called me in for a briefing to inform me that I had just volunteered to be a radio jammer. He also explained that I would be transferred immediately to Hawaii. Lastly, he told me that because of the secrecy of my new duties that I would not be allowed to carry my service records with me. He told me that my official Navy records would indicate that I was still attending the radio technician's school on Treasure Island.

I didn't care about any of that. All I was thinking about was how relieved I was that I wasn't in trouble again.

CHAPTER FIFTEEN

YOU DON'T WANT TO KNOW!

I shipped out almost immediately to Iroquois Point Amphibious Assault Base on the island of Oahu in Hawaii. But before shipping out, my commanding officer told me that if any other officer asked me what I did, the standard reply should be:

"You don't want to know."

I said that many times and never got another question from any officer. It was like the code word used by patrons to get into my parents' speakeasy back home.

A Limey (English commando) trained me to swim ashore and how to kill any Japanese soldiers who were on beach patrol. The Limey also told me why we did not want to have our service records with us in combat. He swam ashore for the first time in France. Allied forces air dropped radio equipment for him to carry to the "fifth column," otherwise known as the underground resistance movement. He also had instructions on how to contact the resistance fighters. Shortly after he began his first radio transmission, a German soldier who spoke English very well got on his radio frequency and told him that the German army already knew that he was on the ground in France. The German soldier also informed Limey that his own mother had been hit by a bus back in England. He further informed Limey that his father had just had a heart attack as a result of the bus accident. Of course, the Limey told me that none of these things were actually the truth.

But that was the last time the Limey carried his service records on an infiltration mission even though he swam ashore on France two more times. Spies are good at getting into military records.

While training in Hawaii, I swam ashore on several nearby islands just for practice. Each time, the Limey praised me. He was amazed that I could slip up on him in the jungle. The Limey asked me how come I knew how to get along so well ashore. I told him that my grandmother had trained me in the Indian ways. She was a full-blooded Oglalla Sioux. As a young maiden, she had been stolen away from her tribe by a band of Cherokee warriors avoiding the pursuing Sioux who had returned and found out about the young girls being kidnapped. The Cherokees took the girls to a city in Missouri where they were sold off of a stump. She was bought by my grandfather, an Englishman, Jerome Chester Chamberlin, who ran drayage wagons. She was his wife and went to school to learn to read and write. This way she could help him in the business.

It is clear to me now why grandma was always playing with me and held me on her lap telling me the stories an Indian boy should know. When I had my seizures, she helped take care of me. She even went camping with us. My family went camping so often, sometimes fishing and drying the fish, sometimes picking wild berries or other edible plants. My brothers, however, do not remember being told any Indian stories.

Today, I wish I could still remember all of the stories about behavior patterns that my grandmother taught me. Many of them were about young boys and how they could take care of themselves in the woods. She would tell me a story and then I would have to repeat it back to her word for word every time she would ask me about it. If I made any errors, she would correct me and make me repeat the story without any errors.

CHAPTER SIXTEEN

CHOICES

Following the many wartime incidents previously recorded, and immediately following my honorable discharge from the U.S. Navy, I returned to the San Francisco Bay Area where I intended to start college at Berkeley, California. But July 26 rolled around, and that was my mother's birthday. I decided, even though I was already registered for classes starting in September, I would make the trip back to Portland, where my mother lived so that we could celebrate her birthday properly.

During the time I spent in Portland, a Saturday night came along. I began to reminisce about the charge that Socks, one of my Navy buddies, had given to the men of our unit: "If I don't return, one of you must go to church for me."

I decided to fulfill his wish and go to church once for Socks.

However, I had to think it through and do it on my own terms. I did not want to pretend that I was a goody little boy doing his duty. So I decided to go to a church where they would most likely know who I was. That way, surely they would know me and my reputation. I was pretty sure I could fight my way out afterwards even if the church gang outnumbered me. I figured the men would most likely jump me and try to teach me a lesson.

I told mother I would attend church in the morning. She surprised me when she announced she was going to accompany me. Thinking back on it, I am sure that she figured if she attended church with me, then the church men would never attack us.

The service was conducted by a young man wearing the robe of someone who had earned a master's degree. I had recently attended a graduation ceremony in Berkeley and I noticed that the master's degree robe is unmistakable because it has these short extensions under the arms. Although I recognized the robe, I can not tell you a single thing the man said during the entire service.

But I did notice that even though it wasn't hot in the church, for some strange reason my mother and I were just perspiring and wiping the sweat beads off of our foreheads like crazy.

When the speaker ended, he abruptly walked down the aisle towards us while he pronounced a benediction with arms outstretched. I thought he looked like a science fiction creature flapping his wings and flying down the aisle.

My mom and I both hoped to make a quick exit, but the preacher had the doorway cut off. And lots of people immediately started crowding around him. We thought they were getting ready to jump us. We were seated at the back of the sanctuary on a pair of folding chairs. I figured if I couldn't handle things myself and my mother was in any sort of danger at all from these folks, then I could just break out a window with one of the folding chairs. I would put her out first, then get out myself.

Some men started making their way toward me so I moved away from them and placed a few empty chairs between them and myself. Then I noticed my mother successfully make it past the group standing at the door. She had just walked outside! I glanced quickly around and finally saw a chance for my own escape. I dashed past the last couple of worshipers who were visiting with the preacher.

I had made it!

I was heading down the long sidewalk towards Cully Road and the gas station at a lively trot when a voice suddenly called out to me.

"Cliff!" the voice said. "Cliff! Stop! It's Conrad!"

Conrad was the only person from my hometown that I had met during the war. He was from my old neighborhood. I bumped into him

Choices

while passing through Guam towards the end of the war. I had stopped at the mess hall for supper on Agana Air Base when all of a sudden a voice hailed me. It was Conrad. He had mess hall duty and was serving guys standing in another line. After filling my tray, I claimed a table then went back to where Conrad was working. I moved aside a couple of sailors who were patiently waiting for their food, then Conrad and I started talking.

I remember thinking that the sailors were preparing to say something to me about moving them along. But apparently they took one look at me dressed in combat fatigues with the sleeves cut off of my uniform shirt and a K-bar knife strapped to my leg. The sailors quickly reconsidered, and gave us all the space I demanded.

Conrad and I quickly agreed to meet each other after he finished his assigned duty. I finished my chow, and then went to talk with his boss. I lied to the mess sergeant when I told him that Conrad and I were old friends. Actually, we barely knew each other and I think the mess sergeant surmised as much. But the sergeant took a careful look at me.

"Sailor, what do you do?" he asked me, looking me up and down.

"You don't want to know," I told him.

He immediately gave Conrad the rest of the day off, as well as the entire next day.

As you can tell, I was accustomed to getting my own way even in the military.

For the rest of that afternoon and evening, Conrad and I sat on a grassy knoll just staring out at the open sea. We talked for hours about our old neighborhood and the grade school which we had both attended even though Conrad and I had not been friends during that period of time. He was associated with the church. And I was from the speakeasy. He, too, was from a well-to-do family. I remembered that Conrad's grandfather had presented him with a nice car just as Conrad started high school. He was handsome, with black hair. But I think the girls were crazy about Conrad mostly because he had a car.

One memory we did share, however. Years before, some friends and I managed to get our hands on a half-gallon of beer. We were drinking it as we sat in front of a neighborhood grocery store late one night. Conrad came along at about that same time and indicated that he wanted to join our little party. I kicked his ass and sent him home.

He and I laughed about that same incident during our long night together on Guam. Conrad said then that he still remembered the beating I gave him many years ago. But he was still his usual friendly self towards me.

I then told Conrad of another experience one time when I flew into Guam on my way to Hawaii. Many Japanese prisoners of war were being held on Guam where they were allowed to help with the landscaping or cleaning up of trash from along the roadsides. I usually felt ill at ease whenever the Japanese prisoners were around. Many times they trimmed grass and shrubbery with the smooth swings of a long machete. I could imagine one of them chopping off my head in a single stroke if he knew what I had been doing to his countrymen.

This particular time, however, one of the Japanese prisoners—most likely an interpreter—was being informally questioned by a marine guard as to how and where he had learned English. The Japanese prisoner indicated that he had attended California State University (CAL) at Berkeley. When he went back to trimming shrubbery, I approached the prisoner and asked him once again if he had really attended CAL. He said "Yes" in probably better English than I spoke.

I then went to the marine guard and asked if I could have that "Jap." The guard looked at me standing there in my combat gear for a minute until he finally said,

"OK. Where will you be?"

"In the mess hall right over there," I replied.

"You'll have to have him back in two hours." the guard told me

When the two of us walked into the mess hall, a sailor came up to me and said:

"No Japs allowed in here!"

I rose slowly into a combat stance. The sailor took one look at me and then simply turned around and left the building.

The Japanese prisoner and I sat and talked about college. We also drank some coffee. It was very strange to be sitting there chatting casually with someone that my instincts told me was supposed to be my enemy.

Choices

But I was very curious about college. In the radio technician program, everybody else had some college training before they enlisted. That is, everyone except me. I liked the radio technicians who had attended Berkeley. After speaking with the likes of those men, I was resolved to go there myself once the war ended and I was discharged.

CHAPTER SEVENTEEN

PRESIDENT ROOSEVELT'S PRAYER

These thoughts and more flooded my brain when Conrad stopped me outside while I was leaving the church. He invited me to join him at the Christian Endeavor group meeting that same afternoon. He indicated the church group was sponsoring an informal outing down by the Columbia River. I told Conrad that I was intending merely to go home, take a bath, and put on a fresh change of clothing. I neglected to mention to Conrad that I was still dripping wet with sweat from the church service. After my anticipated bath, I informed Conrad, I was planning a visit to the Big Apple, a local tavern, with the full intention of getting drunk.

"No," he said forcefully. "We need to talk. And besides, you'll have a lot more fun with our church's youth group."

Again, I declined his invitation as politely as I knew how.

"I'll come by and pick you up," he insisted.

"Don't bother," I told Conrad bluntly.

"I'll see you soon," he continued, seemingly deaf to my repeated resistance. "I know you don't have any wheels, so just wait at home for me," he concluded.

I went straight home. As soon as my mother came out from her bath, I went in. I was ringing wet with sweat and it wasn't even a very warm day. When I came out from the bath with just slacks on, there was Conrad seated in the living room waiting for me.

It seems there was nothing else to do but go with him to the river. Conrad bragged me up something fierce during the outing. He told everyone in the Christian Endeavor group that he had seen me swim across the mile-wide mouth of the Columbia River from Washington state to Oregon state just a few years before. But he failed to mention the main reason for my swim. There was a lot of money riding on whether I would make it all the way across. Conrad did not know this because all the bets had been laid on at my mom's saloon. Many of her patrons thought that I wouldn't make it past the busy shipping channel that runs down the center of the Columbia River.

So I went to the river outing with Conrad and we had a great time. We all had a swim and a picnic, then we headed back to the church for a Christian Endeavor meeting.

Reluctant to enter the church a second time, I tried to express my fears. But Conrad didn't seem to understand. He thought I was joking. The young people talked to me and asked if I was staying. They even invited me to the young adults' Sunday school class that met at 9:30 A.M. the next week.

At the conclusion of the Christian Endeavor meeting that Sunday night, each of the participants prayed out loud and shared their individual problems. The last thing they did was to begin sentence prayers. I could tell they were taking turns going up and down all the rows. They finally got to me, and I think I shocked them all when I prayed President Roosevelt's prayer!

I had committed it to memory during the war.

Back then, a group of us on Iwo Jima had gathered around a young marine who was obviously badly wounded and dying. Blood was burbling out of his mouth whenever he tried to talk. But before he finally died, he managed to say to no one in particular:

"Pray for me!"

Those of us helping him looked at each other and shrugged. None of us were the praying kind. Finally, one guy turned to me.

"You pray for him, Lucky. You always have the words!" he said.

President Roosevelt's Prayer

Never in my whole life to that point had I ever uttered a single prayer. I didn't know the first thing about praying. But I was determined never to let that happen to me again. I dug deep down into my pack where I knew I carried a New Testament with the Psalms. Every person in military service was issued one, whether they thought they needed it or not.

In the back of that booklet was the Lord's Prayer. Right underneath it was President Roosevelt's signature. If it was good enough for the President of the United States, I figured it was good enough for that dying marine. I memorized it on the spot.

Well, the sentence prayers at Conrad's church were going up and down the rows and finally came to me, so I began praying.

"Our Father...."

To my surprise, they all joined in unison. How did they all knew President Roosevelt's prayer, I wondered. Returning home quite confused, I was growing more and more curious as to what this church thing was all about.

I thought about Socks and how he never went out drinking and carousing with the rest of us. Shoot, Socks was never even in the brig like the rest of us had been at least once each. I thought about how close I came to being convicted of assaulting an officer and going to Leavenworth federal prison. I decided right then I needed to know more of what the church was all about. And I wondered how long it would take me to find that out.

With pre-registration forms for the next semester at CAL-Berkeley already completed, a return trip in just three short weeks was inevitable. In the meantime, I remained in Portland to look up some old friends and drink a bit with each of them. They were all talking about attending college or going on and on about their jobs.

They all seemed so settled down compared to how they had acted in the good old days before the war. Many of them were already married, and a few that I thought would never join that institution were on the verge of marriage.

Determined to find out more about the church, I continued attending services at Acreage Presbyterian. I also bought myself a Bible and began to read it.

Time passed all too quickly. Soon it was time for me to go back to California and get on with my college education. I had only completed two years of high school and ended up quitting in the fall of my third year. I had worked for a while before enlisting in the Navy, quite by accident.

Back at CAL-Berkeley, I soon discovered that I had enrolled in a class but couldn't remember what course it was. A professor looked through the registration cards and told me there were some students enrolled in his classes who had never completed the proper prerequisite courses. One of those cards might belong to me, I thought to myself. The professor told me that if I had any further questions, I should simply come by his office and make an appointment to see him. Later that same day, the professor's secretary indicated it would be some time during the next semester before the professor would have any appointment time available.

That blew me away.

Everything seemed to be going wrong. After just two weeks at CAL, I dropped out and moved back to Portland. Conrad had told me earlier that a lot of service men and women were going to Vanport on the GI Bill. Vanport was an extension campus set up because there was such a flood of ex-GI's starting college. If you attended Vanport, then you were automatically tied into later enrollment at either the University of Oregon in Eugene or Oregon State College, now also a university, in Corvallis. All course credits issued by Vanport were completely transferable to the other two schools.

Once again I looked up Conrad, and then I bought myself a car.

College registration was just a few days away. I went out to Vanport and was inundated with the numbers of students and decisions on what courses to take. I told the registration clerk of my desire to become an electrical engineer. But after completing a few engineering classes, I soon discovered that mathematics was my real forte.

Continuing to read my Bible at night, I also attended Acreage Presbyterian Church each Sunday. I went to the adult Sunday school class, Sunday morning services and Christian Endeavor (CE) meetings on Sunday evenings. But studying and reading more of the Bible just caused me to become more and more frustrated. In particular, I was

President Roosevelt's Prayer

uncomfortable at the CE meetings whenever the young people would take turns praying. By this time I had learned that the prayer I memorized during the war was actually The Lord's Prayer, and invariably it would be recited at the end of each meeting.

The minister at Acreage Presbyterian was an old man with a white beard. He would always begin our conversations together by asking the same question.

"Are you about ready to give your life to Christ and join the church?" the minister would ask me.

My standard reply to his question was that I was still reading the Bible.

CHAPTER EIGHTEEN
ASK CLIFF TO PREACH

The old minister at Acreage Presbyterian eventually went back into retirement after a younger man who had just graduated from seminary became the new minister. It wasn't too long after the younger man joined us that I began to feel as if I ought to preach. The young preacher did not really know much about the real world and what it was like. For my money, he did not drive the points of salvation and redemption home hard enough.

Mind you, although still not converted, I was already starting to think about how to prepare a sermon.

Well, you probably will not believe this, but one Saturday night the young minister's wife called and told me that her husband, Harry, had laryngitis. He had apparently written her a note directing her to ask Cliff to preach.

"I'm not converted! Why me?" I asked her.

She replied that she did not know, for the life of her, why me either. She told me that she had tried to argue with her husband about my ability to preach, but to absolutely no avail.

You guessed it! I did preach.

I told everyone in that congregation how they were all sinners. I told them I knew all of their secrets and had seen how they behaved with their neighbors. When I finished preaching, I went to the door at the back of the sanctuary and prepared to greet them as they filed past me. But no one said a word! Finally, one of the church leaders, an elder, quietly told me:

"It's a good thing we took the offering first! If we had waited until after the sermon, I don't believe we would have received a single cent!"

Since that experience, the practice in my own ministry—as much as it was in my power to do so—was never to take an offering before the sermon.

The retired minister, Henry Hampton, still lived in the area so I went to see him. Whenever you went to Henry's house, it was an experience in itself. Any visitors were always seated in the formal living room. There, they would be served hot tea by his wife. Finally, the visitor gained an audience with the Reverend Hampton.

My visit that day began by asking him, "How do you know if God is calling you or speaking to you?"

Recounting my various experiences so far, I also noted my confusion with what I was hearing from preachers on the radio and at various Christian Endeavor conferences. They all seemed to know without any doubt that God had told them to raise money for this or that, or to do some other outlandish thing.

"How can you tell when it is God speaking and not your own desires?" I wanted to know.

His answer, it seemed, was of no real help to me at that point in my faith. He told me, "God never tells you something until he first tells someone else the same thing."

His statement did not provide me with much comfort, but it did remind me of something that a young adult Sunday school teacher by the name of Ruth Lee had told me only a few days before:

"When God calls you, Clifford, remember what Isaiah said: 'Here I am Lord..' "

Ruth Lee then informed me that she knew God was calling me.

Several nights later, while I was upstairs in my mother's house, I got this strange feeling. Either I had to quit all this church stuff and quit reading the Bible, or I had to accept Jesus as my personal savior.

Ask Cliff to Preach

First, I threw my Bible on the floor. Then I retrieved it. I made my decision that very night in that cold upstairs room. I dropped to my knees and accepted Jesus as my personal Savior. To this day, I have never been sorry. I have never looked back.

In addition, I went on to major in mathematics in college and even completed some graduate school courses. My goal was to teach mathematics in a university. But that wasn't God's goal for my life.

CHAPTER NINETEEN

A REAL JOB OFFER? BAH!

While attended graduate school at what is now Oregon State University in Corvallis, one memory stands out from all others.

We were supposed to pick a project, work it up and turn it in for our course grade. I chose to do some language experimentation with differential equations. I already had some familiarity with cryptography due to my work in the Navy. Although I had not specifically been trained to service the Navy's code machines, most shipboard officers assumed that all radio technicians were able to do anything. Twice, while aboard big ships, I had serviced the code machines. Well, I completed my graduate school project and received an "A" grade for the class. But I never received back my term paper describing the project. When I questioned the professor, he said that he had sent it to a friend of his who worked in that particular field.

Art Milne, PhD, was head of the mathematics department at Oregon State University. He called me in to his private office and told me that I had a chance for a job interview with the government. He indicated that I should go to the interview even if I had no interest in the job because it would be good experience.

On the appointment day, I went down to the Benson Hotel in Portland and met a man who was interviewing all mathematics majors.

Much to my surprise, the government jobs recruiter held in his hand my term paper on cryptography. He told me that he could not return it to me because the paper had things in it that were considered classified information. The recruiter then offered me a chance to go to cryptography school in Maryland with a super job at the conclusion.

I looked around the hotel room and noticed a second man who looked to me more like some kind of hoodlum. I could see the second man was wearing a tailor-made suit jacket cut large enough to hide a barely concealed .357 magnum and shoulder holster.

I asked my interviewer who the second man was.

"He's my bodyguard," the interviewer simply said.

The government recruiter informed me that if I went to cryptography school, then at some point a bodyguard would be assigned to me as well. By that time, he indicated, I would have access to confidential information at the most secret levels and therefore would need the protection that only a personal bodyguard could offer. He concluded by saying that his own bodyguard even slept in the same room with him and his wife.

Wow! I wasn't married, but I could never conceive of such a thing.

I told him right then and there that I was not interested in cryptography school or in any other part of his job offer. That is when he started to become rather threatening. He told me that the military might draft me. At that point, attending cryptography school might well seem preferable to service in the armed forces, he said.

I responded that I was no longer subject to the draft because of my previously completed military service.

"Sometimes they make mistakes and draft you again," he cautioned.

Countering his not-so veiled threats, I declared myself to be a good Democrat who had already received help for his mother from our Congressman. He returned tit for tat. He said he had already checked me out. He informed me that he knew I had a very high security clearance during the war.

A Real Job Offer? Bah!

I refused his offer of training and employment, but for many years afterwards the government continued to bug me about attending cryptography school until I finally graduated from seminary.

Finally, it was time to quit graduate school. Traveling to Hong Kong interested me as I heard business was booming over there. I wanted nothing to do with cryptography school. After attempting to teach mathematics at the university level, my conclusion was that I hated it. Some of my students were too dumb to understand what was being taught. Others were too cocky. When errors were pointed out, they just wanted to argue.

It was at about this same time in my life that I met Eulalie, whom I eventually married. My life was finally starting to come together following many years of seeming as if it was falling apart. Eulalie was just what was needed to make my life meaningful. No longer did I feel the need to leave the country for Hong Kong. Eulalie and I met just before spring vacation. Each of us fell madly in love with the other. I would have preferred to make her a June bride, but her mother was horrified by the thought of such a short romance.

When Eulalie and I first met, she was a beautiful woman. I still think she is beautiful today! She stood 5-feet, 6-inches, weighed 120 pounds, and is nearly seven years younger than I am. She had dark brown hair, brown eyes and was light-skinned even though she is 1/16th Native American. Her nickname when we met was "Pete." She had been dating Mike, one of my friends from college who was recruited for the Oregon State College basketball team because he stood 7-feet, 1-inch.

But Mike couldn't catch a basketball to save his life. He lived in Lake Oswego, and introduced me to Eulalie during one of our trips. Since I had a car, I would drive Mike and another basketball player from Corvallis, where we were all in school, to a home outside Portland where Mike's parents lived. After meeting his parents on one such trip, Mike suggested we go meet Pete, whom I took to be one of his many boyhood friends.

Boy, was I in for a surprise!

Pete turned out to be Eulalie.

Shortly after we met, Eulalie and I attended a dance at Oregon State College. We still laugh today—some 56 years later—about how all of my friends took turns complimenting me on her good looks. One fellow told me he would have married her himself if I hadn't landed her first.

Among her many other skills, Eulalie could play the piano quite well. Since I can't carry a tune in a bucket, we made a good worship team.

Even today, I believe we make a perfect team!

CHAPTER TWENTY

SEMINARY

To appease Eulalie's mother, we agreed to marry in September. Before we said our vows, however, I told my bride-to-be that seminary might be in my future plans. Eulalie was elated. I still held firmly to my convictions that a preacher ought to know something about the real world, but I know now that seminary would never have been in the cards if Eulalie and I had not married.

My Presbytery committee on pastoral candidates would not allow me to attend McCormick Seminary in Chicago, which was my desire. The committee members all said that I was too worldly already and did not need to be further influenced by a worldly seminary. According to them, what I needed was a spiritual experience such as that offered by San Francisco Theological Seminary in San Anselmo, where Jesse Baird could look after me.

Jesse Hays Baird was president of San Francisco Theological Seminary while I attended there. He was a man who stood well over six feet tall. He would sometimes meet me after class and walk down the hall with his arm around my shoulders. At 5-feet, 7 1/2-inches, I could easily fit under his arm. While we walked, he would tell me to be patient with my professors and fellow students who seemed snobbish. He would often tell me that I was going to be a sawdust trail evangelist, just has he had been.

He had an honorary doctoral degree and was likely named president of the seminary because he was so successful in raising money. Other professors were sometimes overheard putting Jesse Baird down because of his honorary doctorate. But to me, Jesse Baird was a real Christian. He knew the very date when he accepted Jesus as his Savior. And he was never ashamed to tell others about it.

Other students did not receive me well at the seminary. My conversion experience had happened less than three years before my start in seminary. And it was just four years since my final amphibious landing and my last combat victim. The tension I felt at seminary was pretty rough. Due to my wartime experiences, I still slept each night with one hand touching a rifle—bayonet fixed—that each night rested on the floor just underneath my bed. My nerves were so frayed that I would fight just about anyone at the drop of a hat.

Eulalie was already bugging me about keeping a loaded rifle under the bed. In addition, our house also held a shotgun, a twenty-two rifle and a pistol in a holster.

But she left me alone in the end.

Even while attending seminary, I continued to work full-time on the outside. I operated a mobile roadside service for vehicles that broke down while traveling on Highway 101. Providing services for building contractors was another sideline business of mine. The contractors often needed emergency repairs late at night at the large housing tracts they were constructing near the seminary.

Working both jobs began to really bother my back after awhile. Apparently, laying on my back—either on a wheeled creeper or just on bare concrete—while doing auto repairs was causing damage to my muscles and bones. Eventually, I closed both businesses.

The next job I took involved teaching mathematics and English at the College of Marin, as well as some classes for inmates at San Quentin Penitentiary. But then came the usual round of state budget cuts for classes and programs considered superfluous.

Administrators eventually decided to reduce the number of mathematics and English classes offered at the community college. That was a ridiculous decision, in my opinion, but I couldn't fight the entire state of California by myself. Rather than lose too many work hours, I became a prison guard at San Quentin.

Seminary

Partly because of my outside work during seminary, I was always able to buy new cars every other year. This, I soon discovered, also did not endear me to my classmates, many of whom could not afford to keep even a used car in operation.

It really amazed that they were so easily offended.

One friend I made while attending seminary was Bill Wartes. He was helping organize a new church in Marin City while still attending seminary classes. Bill and his wife, Bonnie, lived on a small income. One day, Eulalie and I went to the grocery store and on our way home decided to stop briefly and visit with the Wartes. After our brief stay, we continued home but accidentally forgot to retrieve our grocery bag containing steaks and other meal staples from their kitchen counter.

When Eulalie finally remembered where we had left our groceries, she called Bonnie Wartes and was surprised when Bonnie repeatedly said thank you.

It seems that the Wartes had not eaten steak in several years.

Eulalie and I laughed at the misunderstanding and wished them well with our unintended gift of food.

My worldliness got me into trouble in other ways, particularly when one student stood up in one of my classes and announced to the others that, in his opinion, no one whose father or grandfather had not been a Presbyterian minister should be admitted to the seminary.

That got my ire up! He was standing right there in front of me, so I stood up as well and said to him,

"I suppose that includes me?"

Turning around slowly he said, "Especially you!"

With that remark I decked him! I hit him so hard, I knocked him through two rows of students still seated in front of us. It seemed like boot camp all over again. I ended up in the vice president's office with several professors standing around and all lamenting that no one could remember anything like this ever happening during the seminary's entire 75-year history.

My mentor, seminary president Jesse Hays Baird was out of town raising funds at the time, so the vice president and several professors decided to send me home without making any decision as to whether the seminary should dismiss me.

They simply told me not to talk to anyone about the incident.

"What would happen," they cautioned me, "if others took out their anger or frustration as I had done?"

On his return, president Jesse Baird looked me up once again in one of the crowded hallways between classes. He put his big bear of an arm around me and told me once more that I was destined to be a sawdust trail evangelist just as he had been.

He repeatedly tried to tone me down.

But upon my return to class, I continued to preach and convert the other students and professors. Otherwise, they were heading straight for hell, I figured.

For my efforts at evangelism, I was reproached many times by seminary professors in the hall. Some students were afraid of me and would leave angry notes. Others would run by going the opposite direction and shout:

"You belong at Berkeley Baptist."

To this day, I do not remember the name of the student whom I hit in class at seminary. But I continued to inquire about him whenever I attended Synod meetings, gatherings of church leaders from throughout a several state territory. Eventually, I learned that the young man had left the ministry just three years after completing his seminary training.

I could identify with his sense of frustration. My own doubts bothered me for many years after seminary. I wondered if I had indeed made the right decision.

Shortly after my fight in the classroom, a distinguished member of the Presbyterian Church's Board of National Missions came to visit our seminary. During his visit, Dr. J. Earl Jackman had me summoned to his presence.

Earl Jackman headed up the national denomination's Sunday School Missions, Mobile Ministries and mission work in Alaska.

"When you graduate, I will have a field for you," Earl Jackman said to me. "You are my kind of man."

Earl Jackman was born in 1900 into a large family. His father was disabled, and his mother struggled to support all of her children by teaching school. However, she did not yet have her teaching credential so her pay was low. She attended classes each summer in an effort to earn her teaching credential. She was proud that her son had gone

Seminary

off to college. He had worked his way through school. Earl Jackman was not much taller than 5-feet, 8-inches tall, but he always dressed in a suit, shirt and tie, and wore a hat, overcoat and gloves. He would dress that way even when he later joined me to visit lumber camps and logging operations.

Bill Wartes was a seminary classmate of mine who ended up serving as a missionary in Alaska where Dr. Jackman had occasion to visit more than once in the course of his duties. Bill Wartes was a bush pilot, and on at least one visit had flown Earl Jackman into a remote part of Alaska in a small float plane. Before the plane reached shore, however, Earl Jackman stepped out of the plane's cabin and into about three feet of ice-cold Arctic sea water. Earl Jackman waded ashore in his suit and street shoes.

Earl Jackman was like a father to me. He was so patient with my tendencies toward violence. After my graduation from seminary, he loved to hear my stories of the really large loggers and mill workers who I baptized on my missionary field.

Earl Jackman carried a little black book everywhere he went. He would often make notes in it as he traveled. All of those working under his guidance would, from time to time, receive notes penned while he was flying across the country from one end to another. If Earl Jackman was known for anything, he was known for that little black book and his patient faith in Jesus.

I did not think much more about my encounter with Earl Jackman until much later when I went as a candidate seeking a youth ministry job at a big church in Portland.

An elder on the church's Pastor Nominating Committee called me aside and told me he would be voting against the church calling me to the position. He told me it was because he had heard about some of the things in my past and about the attitude I exhibited while attending seminary.

Well, I left town never to hear from that church ever again.

You must realize there was a critical need for seminary graduates in the Presbyterian Church at that time. Most seminary graduates had multiple job offers. Often, they had the luxury of choosing among calls from several different churches.

But not me!

Obviously, even though I had kept my end of the bargain and remained quiet about the seminary classroom incident in which I had decked another student, the secret was not so closely kept by others who had taught at or attended the seminary.

Eventually, seminary president Jesse Baird sent me a note informing me about a new ministry in the California lumber town of Burney, about 40 miles east of Redding. It was to be a ministry of tent evangelism to the many lumber camps, sawmills and itinerant groups of construction workers. Eulalie and I drove up to the area for a visit. There we found a few Christians living in the general area as well as two or three Sunday schools supervised by laymen.

"What a challenge!" I thought to myself.

We took the job and went there for a promised salary of $3,300 per year.

My annual earnings had been twice that amount while working part-time and attending seminary. It was three years later when I finally learned that the people from Big Bend, another nearby community, had voted against my coming there. To this day, forty years after our arrival and long after my retirement from the ministry, we still have friends living in those same communities. Recently we were invited back to the community for a going away party being given upon the departure of one of the old timers in Big Bend. What a joyous occasion that was to behold!

CHAPTER TWENTY-ONE

TURKEY SHOOT

When Eulalie and I first moved to Big Bend, California, there were ex-convicts living there who recognized me from my prison guard duties at San Quentin Penitentiary. I was given a wide path by these men who often drank their beer while sitting on the steps of the community store. I was remembered from San Quentin as an officer who had fired his gun to quell a disturbance, and a guard who was never slow to use his baton. There was a wide path given, but no real respect shown nor the trading of casual conversation.

Soon after we moved there, I noticed an announcement on the community bulletin board of a turkey shoot scheduled for a Fourth of July celebration to be held at the community club. I had recently purchased a new Winchester 30-30 rifle for deer hunting, and I was anxious to try it out. My stepfather, an infantry sergeant, long ago had taught me to shoot. He had represented the U.S. Army as a sharpshooter in several international competitions. Using the techniques he taught me, I also had competed once in a junior-level meet sponsored by the National Rifle Association. One of the things my step-father taught me was how to control my breathing so shots could be squeezed off without losing my aim. But I was not considered an outstanding marksman by any stretch of the imagination.

Early on the appointed morning, I went to the turkey shoot and signed up for the first competition of the day. All of the hunter-types welcomed my dollar and reckoned me for an easy mark. I could hear them snickering at me.

"Let's take the preacher's dollar," they said.

Well, when it came time for me to shoot, I was surprised to find that we would be shooting at a large, three-foot high, target at a distance of 100 yards. The target was set up a hill at least 30 feet higher than the ground on which we stood to shoot. Target shooters do not usually shoot uphill because of the effects of gravity on a traveling bullet. There was a board set up between two trees that made a table for the list of shooters. The shooter was to stand behind the table and shoot off hand.

Wow! I thought. This would be pretty tough.

My turn came at what looked like a real gamble. I guessed the target course was designed to favor hunters who usually shoot off hand at a deer standing slightly up hill from the hunter's own position. I practiced my breathing and squeezed off my first shot. The man marking the target popped his head up and signaled a hit. Then he let out a real loud, "Whoop!" Well, when all the men had shot, the target came down and my number was on a hole just touching the "X" at the target's very center. I had the competition's only "10" score.

I won the first turkey and the men said, "What a lucky shot the preacher got off!" Then they laughed derisively.

As the event organizers began promoting their second competition for a turkey, they came to me and said that I ought to kick in again. After all, they argued, hadn't I already picked out the largest turkey from those staked out for the winners to take home. I put up another dollar just to keep them quiet. So then they kidded me and asked if I intended to win the second round as well.

It struck me that it was not my own skill that allowed me to shoot as successfully as I had. Rather, the Holy Spirit had something in mind for these folks. I told the contest organizers that apparently God was on my side. They laughed as they walked off. When it came my turn on the second turkey I again looked at the impossible shot and expected to get a score of "8," at best.

Turkey Shoot

I practiced my breathing and heard some derisive talk about the preacher until some of the men in charge of the contest quieted all of the spectators. I squeezed off what I thought was a good shot but had no faith in another "X."

When the target finally came down at the end of that round, my number was on another "X." The second turkey was also mine.

Praising the Lord for everyone to hear, I was greeted only by silence on the part of those really rough men who thought of themselves as great hunters.

I went to select the second turkey, but on the walk over to where the live birds were penned I decided to donate this one back to the community club so that those who wanted to do so could shoot for it again. When I came back to the area where the turkey shoot was held, bar owner Jack Hayes took me aside and said,

"Preacher, I don't think you ought to sign up for the next shoot because we can't get very many of the others to sign up for it if you are going to compete."

Instead, he suggested I wander over to the area where the women were shooting 22s for chickens. But the women over there did not want me to sign up to shoot either.

It seems that the two Xs made me a well-known person in the community. The Holy Spirit had used the target shooting competition to make me acceptable as a man. The remainder of the afternoon, the comment I most often overheard was, "The preacher ain't much of a man, but he sure is a hell of a shot."

One of the real hunter-types finally came to me and asked if he could borrow my rifle to shoot for a turkey. His rifle had a telescope sight but he had taped over it. His open sights were not adjusted very well. I loaned my rifle to him but he did not win a turkey with it.

Soon after the July 4 picnic, Jack Hayes (the bar owner) and a man from Pacific Gas & Electric (the local utility) came to the front door of our house. They asked me if I would be interested in serving as scoutmaster of the local Boy Scout troop. They knew that I had been an active Boy Scout leader in the past and a Boy Scout growing up.

The house Eulalie and I rented had a large front porch converted into a sun porch with windows all the way around. That area was my office. Inviting the two men inside, I learned that the community had a small troop of a dozen boys and a committee of men made up from members of the community and Pacific Gas & Electric employees.

I was so new with the Presbyterian Church's Board of National Missions that I had to contact Earl Jackman to inquire whether it would be a conflict of interest to become a scoutmaster. Earl Jackman left it up to me to decide, so I accepted the voluntary position as troop scoutmaster.

CHAPTER TWENTY-TWO
FIRE DANGER!

That first summer in Big Bend, I planned a lot of camping trips with the scout troop. Traveling north from Big Bend was a bridge crossing and a fork in the highway. The branch of highway that forked to the right went on up Nelson Creek. The fork to the left followed Kosk Creek. On one of our Boy Scout trips, we decided to go to Johnson Flat for an overnight. Johnson Flat is a beautiful mountain meadow that can be reached by following the Nelson Creek road. The ground underneath Johnson Flat has a hollow sound to it because of the many volcanic tubes filled with glacial melt water running just beneath the surface.

I pitched my tent, which was actually two shelter halves reclaimed from the military gear issued to me during the war. The equipment had been part of the supplies issued for an amphibious assault.

The scouts and I built our cooking fires and set up our camp. When night came, the boys wanted a troop bonfire. Several of us set to work clearing a large space of bare ground while the remainder of the troop began gathering downed wood. We then built a nice fire.

As we sat there enjoying the flames and embers, a thunderstorm bubbled up complete with loads of thunder and lightning. Some of the scouts were a little scared. I talked to them about the dangers of standing on an exposed hilltop where they might be struck by lightning.

Truthfully, I doubted very much that the boys in my scout troop were in any danger of a lightning strike if we stayed where we were camped. But it was better to warn them just in case the storm moved. Afterwards, I crawled into my GI-issued sleeping bag and soon was fast asleep. Morning arrived before I awoke. The rain had stopped and our fire pit was still warm. As the boys continued to sleep, I began to fix my own breakfast.

The smell of eggs, bacon and flapjacks frying on a hot griddle soon woke everyone else up. The boys all seemed very tired, however. Soon, I learned many of them had stayed awake nearly all night heaping logs up to make a large bonfire. They all smelled pretty smoky, so as soon as we finished breakfast, we cleaned up the area, returned the fire pit to its natural state, and packed up our remaining gear.

We made our way back down to the fork in the road, then decided to go up the Kosk Creek side where we knew there were wide pools ideal for swimming. We went swimming and then made a campsite so we could fix lunch. After lunch, we all headed back to town where I distributed the kids back to their respective homes.

Upon arrival at my own house, my wife Eulalie told me that members of the U.S. Forest Service had come to our house making inquiries as to where I might have taken the Boy Scout troop camping overnight. Because of their concern, I made my way to the forest service district office. The district ranger was away, but returned shortly after I arrived. He told me that a forest service lookout had awakened in the middle of the night and spotted a large blaze. The flames were visible from only one lookout tower, however, so there was no way for the forest service lookouts to determine the fire's exact location.

Men from the forest service had spent the remainder of that night checking all of the surrounding ridge tops for signs of a fire that the lookout guessed may have been started by a lightning strike.

When no forest fire could be found, however, forest service personnel began to wonder if maybe the Boy Scouts had been up on Johnson Flat with a large bonfire. They had actually gone up there to check, but returning crew members reported no signs of the troop campsite or a large bonfire.

Fire Danger!

It was only at that point in their narrative that I volunteered information about what had happened and how the boys, scared by lightning and thunder, had kept a large bonfire blazing for many hours after I had gone peacefully to sleep.

Even thirty years later, my forest service friends and I laugh together about the stormy night when I was able to slumber so well.

CHAPTER TWENTY-THREE

"FIFTEEN TWO! FIFTEEN FOUR!"

Mrs. Browning, mother of one of the youngest Boy Scouts in my new troop, would walk with her son down to the community hall every time he came to the meetings. Afterwards, she would meet him and walk him home. The other boys came by themselves, or their parents drove them to the meetings.

Very shortly after I met her at the first scout meeting, Mrs. Browning requested that I visit her. She said there was something she needed to tell me. At the earliest opportunity, I went to her cabin, but she only nervously asked me about the various major league baseball teams. Very soon after I arrived, Mrs. Browning cut off the conversation, then told me she must go to the store. It was not too difficult to tell that I had been dismissed.

A week later, I returned to Mrs. Browning's home where we enjoyed coffee and small talk until finally she dismissed me once again nervously. Now I was certain that she had something she needed to discuss, but I could not seem to break the ice.

I went a third time to the cabin and this time Mrs. Browning asked me if I played cribbage.

"Sure," I replied.

We sat down with a cribbage board and a deck of cards between us. She began to deal the cards. We played cribbage and as we played, she began to speak very quietly the words for the cribbage game. I took her cue, and as we continued to play, I tried to speak very quietly as well.

Suddenly, and in a much louder voice while we were still playing cribbage she started to talk about many other things on her mind. She started by saying that she made a big mistake once. She told me that she had been drinking and afterwards was driving home with her 15-month-old daughter in the car. She lost control of the vehicle and struck a tree.

"Fifteen two," she said in hushed tones.

Mrs. Browning then continued with the narrative of her long-ago vehicle accident in a much more audible voice. Her infant daughter was hospitalized for more than two weeks during which time Mrs. Browning was detained in the county jail.

"Fifteen two, fifteen four, and the rest do not score," she whispered as the game continued on a different auditory level from her story.

The little girl eventually died from injuries sustained in the accident, and Mrs. Browning was charged with murder.

The district attorney encouraged her to make a deal with the prosecution, so Mrs. Browning pleaded guilty to a single charge of vehicular manslaughter, a misdemeanor. The judge sentenced her to five years probation on the condition that there would be no alcoholic consumption by Mrs. Browning during the entire time of her probationary period. The judge also revoked her driver's license.

Mrs. Browning had grown up in Westwood, Calif., a lumber mill town. She married a logger much older than herself when she was just 17 years old. The couple had two sons, and then finally a little girl was born. Sadly, Mrs. Browning admitted that she started drinking heavily while still a very young woman.

Now here she was, still on probation and prohibited from drinking. Her driver's license would not be reinstated until the end of the five year probationary sentence. Mrs. Browning's husband had worked at one time in Big Bend so he was aware that there was essentially no law enforcement presence in the mountain community miles away from the nearest Shasta County Sheriff's sub-station. I remember one

"Fifteen Two! Fifteen Four!"

meeting I had about that same time period with the sheriff who lived and worked in Redding.

"The people in Big Bend take care of their own problems and we do not need to go in there and interfere," the sheriff had told me.

Figuring that his wife would be unable to halt her drinking habit, Mr. Browning simply moved the family to Big Bend and found a job nearby in the woods. They had lived four years in the town by the time I arrived.

Mrs. Browning said she didn't mind not being able to drive since it was possible to walk everywhere she needed to go in Big Bend. But she did confess that she was still drinking like a fish. Although I was new in town, I did know that Mrs. Browning's best female friend was married to the owner of Big Bend's only bar. The two women were quite a pair.

On at least four other occasions after that visit, Mrs. Browning and I continued to play cribbage. Each game lasted nearly two hours. Gradually, during the course of my visits, we began speaking at a more normal volume when we called our game scores.

As near as I can figure, Mrs. Browning was unable to talk to me about her problems without a cribbage game going on. In this same manner, I was able to cite biblical references to her about the love of God as taught by His son, Jesus. In the beginning, Mrs. Browning believed that she was going to hell for eternity for allowing the incident that lead to the death of her daughter.

From my own understanding of the Bible, I believe that her daughter is already with God, and that she, too, could get herself right with God. Then, she could look forward to meeting her daughter once again in heaven. In her case, I believed that we were making some really good progress in her counseling sessions.

Eventually, I talked to Mrs. Browning's husband, a man who was not ignorant concerning the teachings of Jesus. He had hopes that his wife could be salvaged. He really loved her very much. That is why he had moved the family to Big Bend. Later, they moved away, but I wondered many times afterwards what happened to Mrs. Browning.

About a year after the Browning's moved away, I received a letter from them. Mrs. Browning indicated that they had moved to the California coastal town of Eureka where her husband had found employment in the coastal redwood forests. She also wrote in the same letter that she was able to once again obtain a driver's license.

Near the end of the letter, she thanked me for what she described as "talking her well." But the most gratifying news in the entire letter was a sentence in which Mrs. Browning indicated that she was exploring various churches in Eureka and was trying not to abuse alcohol. Mrs. Browning wrote that she finally believed that she was no longer destined for hell because of the accident.

At about the same time that I graduated from seminary and Eulalie and I moved to Big Bend, a young psychiatrist started his clinical practice at the county's mental health facility in Redding. It wasn't long before the two of us became friends. Whenever I had occasion to be at the county hospital, we would enjoy lunch or a cup of coffee together. Following my receipt of Mrs. Browning's letter, I shared the entire story with my psychiatrist friend. He surmised that the act of playing cribbage was the reality in Mrs. Browning's mind. She was able to share her deep emotional distress only during cribbage games most likely because she rationalized that her confession and our subsequent discussions were done through mental telepathy and, therefore, was unheard by anyone.

CHAPTER TWENTY-FOUR
SNEAKING A PEEK

Besides scouting, there were enough other things to do to keep me occupied. Once, when I returned from a monthly trip to the regional presbytery meeting, I noticed that an old table with just three legs was missing from its usual place in our front yard.

Looking around, I discovered the table had been moved. It was now propped up against an outside wall of our rental house, just underneath the bathroom window. On the table's painted top were the telltale marks of a caulked pair of logger's boots.

My trusty old military rifle immediately came out of the closet. Onto its barrel I fixed a bayonet, and then carried the entire contraption with me as I stomped angrily with a mean purpose down to the nearby bar. My arrival was timed to occur well after the time that I knew the town's men had all returned from their day's work in the woods. In no uncertain words, I told the loggers assembled in the bar that I was hunting for the scoundrel owner of a pair of caulked boots who had been spying on my wife while she was in the shower. Even though the small bar was filled with normally rowdy men, there was not a sound to be heard. I know that I should never have made those threats nor banged the butt of that rifle angrily on the floor of that bar. But I was mad!

Over the years, I have had many opportunities to speak with and counsel men who work in the woods. Often, I would lead a Bible study with men from the local sawmill during their break time. I give all of the credit for any of my successes in reaching those men directly to the Holy Spirit.

While assigned to Big Bend, the most fruitful areas of my ministry were the several lumber camps that I was able to visit. In those days, loggers lived all summer in lumber camps. They worked 10 days straight in the woods, then had four days off. There were no women to be found in camp unless, on rare occasion, there happened to be a woman cook. The bunkhouses and mess hall were all on wooden skis called skids. There usually were a few movable metal maintenance buildings as well. They were periodically moved closer to the work site by towing them with horses, mules, trucks or caterpillar tractors.

Working under those conditions, there were plenty of things for the men to complain about. But the biggest complaints of all were reserved for the frequent lack of days off. The problem, as described to me, had more to do with the periods of each year when the price of lumber soared. That usually coincided with the logging company asking—sometimes demanding—that the men work during some or all of their off days.

Part of my job as a tent evangelist involved periodic visits to each of the logging camps. I would wait for the men to come in from the woods, and then right away I would meet with all of the Christian loggers and share a prayer with them. During this time they often brought up the name of a man who was in that camp and was not yet a Christian. We would pray for him that he would receive the Lord as his personal savior on that very night. After our prayer time, the men would all go off to wash up and prepare for dinner. They had been working hard all day, and they were usually covered with dirt, sawdust, bits of brush, and other forest detritus that clung to their sweat-covered bodies.

CHAPTER TWENTY-FIVE

FIGHT OR RUN, PREACHER!

The Christian loggers would always invite me to stay for dinner with them in the mess hall. Very quickly, I began to notice that the youngest and strongest of them would wolf down their food as rapidly as they possible could. Then, they would take up stations on either side of the mess hall doors. No one was allowed to leave the room, they said.

After the rest of us had finished our meals, several of the non-Christians would attempt to leave because they knew that I would soon be leading a worship service. The frequent skirmishes by the mess hall doors were referred to as exercise time.

That was my cue to stand on one of the tables at the front of the dining hall and commence preaching. About midway through this activity, the second portion of my visit would commence. This usually involved challenges from some of the loggers who would step forward with a menacing look and say to me,

"Fight or run, preacher!"

More often than not, I jumped off the table to wrestle or box with them for a round or two. That is how I earned their respect. When the room quieted down again, I would get back up on a table and continue the worship service. I'm not sure of this, but I often felt that most of the loggers would pull their punches when fighting me.

I say this because it was usually part of a pattern. It did not happen every time. Only occasionally did things get really serious. Particularly if the man who challenged me had been drinking quite a bit before dinner.

But I never fought fair! After all, I had lived through seven potentially deadly Pacific Island invasions where I was surrounded by Japanese soldiers.

My ministry was equipped originally by the Mobile Ministers fund with boxes and boxes of hymnals. But I soon discovered that mimeographed gospel songs were really better received by the men, some of whom could barely read, if at all. During my impromptu worship services, I never used a printed sermon. Bible references were frequent, and I usually spoke for no more than about 10 minutes on any of the scriptures from which I quoted.

Devotions were always followed with an alter call. I can't honestly say that every time an altar call was offered that someone stepped forward. But for the most part, there was almost always someone who came up afterwards to speak with me about problems within his family or to confess his sins.

Arguing theology did not work with any of them. Rather, I was there simply to minister to their needs. I can't remember many of the logging camp's names but I do recall there was Camp Six and another called Whitehorse.

During one of my visits to Camp Six, I was surprised to learn that the old cook had retired. The camp had hired a new woman to do all the cooking. She was a devout Christian, about 40 years old, and extremely heavyset. I'll bet she weighed at least 250 pounds. When I arrived at the camp, she indicated that I was not to start preaching until she could come out of the kitchen.

That particular night, there was some exercise at the doors but the service had not yet started. When the cook finally joined us, she walked up front and thrust her hips from side to side to clear a place on one of the benches up front. As I remember it, a couple of loggers who had been sitting near the front table ended up landing on the floor rather hard.

"I told you to leave me space up front," she said to me.

Fight or Run, Preacher!

No sooner had she seated herself when a red-headed logger named Jim, standing about 5-foot, 9-inches and weighing at least 180 pounds, stood up in the back of the mess hall, took a long pull on a pint of whiskey he was carrying, and came forward with the usual challenge, "Fight or run, Preacher."

Before I could jump off the table and put my Bible down, the cook was on her feet. She grabbed Jim by the shirt, butted him in the forehead with her own head, and let him slump to the bench where she had been sitting quietly just seconds before.

"Jim, you just sit right down here with Ellie. When the time comes, you need to accept the Lord as your Savior tonight," the cook said, loud enough for everyone in the room to hear. She then used her hips to clear a bit more space on the bench until she could sit with one of her arms wrapped around Jim. She held him like that during the entire worship service.

But she had made me mad. I was afraid that the men would act differently toward me since a woman had done the fighting for me. I was stubborn enough in my pride that I wanted to do my own fighting.

That night, I finished my sermon and gave the altar call. The cook simply shoved Jim forward. To my surprise, he kneeled and I prayed for him to receive Jesus as his Savior and Lord. I really wondered if it was the blow to his head, the booze, or both.

To my amazement, when I visited Camp Six the next time, Jim was in the prayer circle and even volunteered to help guard the mess hall doors after dinner. I will never understand the ways of the Lord and how some people come to accept Jesus as the Way, the Truth and the Light. But I have discovered that we are not all the same by any stretch of the imagination.

CHAPTER TWENTY-SIX
EASTER SURPRISE

    A Christian barber in Burney that I frequented for my monthly haircuts learned that I was leading church services in Big Bend and inquired about my pulpit. When he learned that there was no pulpit, he made a portable one for me in his back room wood-working shop. My dear wife, Eulalie, played piano for all of our services in Big Bend. She also had responsibility for our two small children who often accompanied us to services.

    Son Arthur, we called him Art, and daughter Charlotte often would either sit alongside Eulalie at the piano or stand by me holding on to my pants leg. It was all fine with us.

    One particular Sunday morning, as I was preaching in Big Bend, my four-year-old son Art moved from his mother's side to stand by me and hold onto my leg. I was winding up to my finish and didn't notice that Art had ducked his head and stepped in underneath the portable pulpit. He was just tall enough that he could stand erect with his head touching the pulpit's small bookshelf.

    "The Holy Spirit moves men in surprising ways!" I declared loudly, and pounded my hand down on the pulpit. The bookshelf must have bounced into Art's head because immediately afterward he walked off carrying the pulpit. The worshipers all broke into gales of laughter.

I joined in their joyous mood by going immediately into the benediction. Art was a hero for unwittingly taking part in my sermon illustration.

When our first Easter in Big Bend approached, a committee of Christians attending our services met and announced that they wanted to hold a sunrise service. It quickly became a project for the entire community. They decided it would be held in the multipurpose hall at the grade school. As the committee worked, I noticed that some of those involved in the preparations were what might be described as heavy drinkers. They were all regulars, if you will, at the local bar.

Well, Easter Sunday arrived and with it so did I and my family for the community sunrise service. As the doors to the school hall opened , to my utter amazement, standing there on the stage stood a six-foot wooden cross completely covered with beautiful yellow daffodils. Each flower was as fresh as the moment when God made it. The community had done it as a surprise for me. Several people in the know explained that Jack Hayes's wife had headed up the decorations committee. Jack owned the bar and the couple never once made it to church during the entire period of my ministry in the area. The entire community had built the cross and covered it with flowers the day before. To keep the flowers fresh, they placed the flower-covered cross in the bar's cold storage room overnight. Jack and his wife had carried the cross to the school before anyone else was even awake on that Easter morning.

Never since has there been a more joyous moment as the one I felt at that time.

My mind wandered back through the years to my days at the seminary and my protector, president Jesse Baird, and the many times when he would catch up to me in the hall after a class.

Jesse Baird used to tell me that if a person just once in life makes a movement sincerely toward God and his or her fellowmen, then that individual would be saved in the last days. Always I prayed fervently for all those I met along life's pathways that each one of them would take that first step towards God or their neighbor. Prior to that Easter morning, that saying had started sounding as hollow as the old wives tale that whenever a bell rings, an angel gets his or her wings.

Easter Surprise

On that particular Easter Sunday, however, I finally had the opportunity to observe someone who had no prior connection to Jesus Christ or the church making a movement towards God. Such wonder and joy filled my heart at the awesome power of the Holy Spirit and God's never-ending promise of salvation for all those who seek Him.

CHAPTER TWENTY-SEVEN
AN OFFER TO LEAVE

During the period of time that I led services in Big Bend, I enjoyed regular visits from Ruth Maclure, a field representative from the Presbyterian Church's National Board of Education. At that time, I was overseeing six church schools in as many mountain communities. Not surprisingly, quite a bit of my time was spent training church school teachers. Each Church school was scheduled for a different day of the week so that I could attend and teach a class at each. That is why we called them church schools instead of Sunday schools.

On one of her visits, Ruth Maclure expressed an interest in the education work that I was doing. She asked me to dig out the materials I had prepared and go through them with her, explaining how and why various materials had been adapted. She was really pleased with what I was doing. She was also more than a little bit surprised that I had not majored in Christian Education while attending seminary. During her next visit the following year, she stopped by and shared with me the new church school curriculum that had just been developed by the Presbyterian Church.

Ruth Maclure repeated again how much she liked my ideas for adapting all the different curriculum materials used by my diverse church schools. She then asked if I would be interested in writing lessons for the entire Presbyterian denomination.

But I didn't have any spare time since I was teaching and preaching in so many places each week. The travel time alone was really consuming, not to mention the amount of time it took each week to prepare and deliver the sermons, devotional and class lectures.

A few months later, I received a telephone call from a man who introduced himself as a member of the Presbyterian Church's National Board of Education. He informed me that he would be attending the next local meeting of Presbytery, and that he wanted very much to meet with me. We did meet, and he again offered to consider me as a writer for the denomination's new church school materials. Again, I repeated everything I had previously told Ruth Maclure, that I did not have the time.

"If you were selected, we would move you and your family to Philadelphia where you would have a full time job as a curriculum writer," he informed me.

"What is your decision?" he then asked. "And think very carefully about it before you decide what you should do."

Off the top of my head, I agreed to go, but only if they allowed me to practice my lessons in a local Philadelphia church. The practice lessons would need to be with the age group appropriate for the intended curriculum. This was my method for developing ideas.

He seemed really pleased with that response. Several months later, another man called me from Philadelphia to interview me for the job. At that time, I declined the position because I saw myself as an evangelist. I did not feel the Holy Spirit was calling me to this other, rather surprising, offer.

However, my wife and I did agree to train church school teachers throughout northern California. We enjoyed a really full year putting on our traveling training programs for the various Presbyterian churches between San Francisco and the Oregon state line.

That experience helped prepare me for my next assignment, which was to lead a new church development.

CHAPTER TWENTY-EIGHT
NEW CHURCH DEVELOPMENT

Actually, I did two new church development projects in small communities plus an inner city ministry for the Presbyterian Church's Board of National Missions. The first new church development I was assigned to was in Leggett, California.

During that assignment, I received a telephone call informing me of a domestic dispute at the home of one of the families involved in starting the new church. Responding to the call, I went over and started counseling the husband and wife. Working together, we were able to devise a solution to their problem. But when I went outside to get into my car, the husband came out and said to me:

"What you said inside was what we pay you to say. But if you and I were still in the Navy, what would you be saying to me?"

Like me, he had served during World War II.

That disgusted me so much that I almost hit him when he said, "That's what we pay you to say!"

He made me feel as if I had sold my soul. Is that what people thought I was doing? Just saying the words I thought they wanted to hear? Wasn't I walking my talk?

Feeling so defeated by that one statement, I wanted to quit the ministry. The devil took full advantage of that situation. I firmly believed that

From a Speakeasy to the Cross

I was different from every other new church development leader in the Synod. But there I stood filled with so much guilt and shame. I believed at that moment that I had made a huge mistake, one that a real minister would never have made. My guilt reminded me of the time that I fixed that bayonet on my rifle and confronted the loggers in that bar in Big Bend and accused one of them of peeping at my wife in the shower. I felt so unworthy that I briefly considered demitting the ministry. I even looked up how to go about it in the Presbyterian Church's official Book of Order, Chapter 7, Section 2, Paragraph 4b.

But I didn't do it.

CHAPTER TWENTY-NINE
A VISION OF JESUS

A few days later, in the middle of another week, I was standing alone in the middle of a residence in Leggett that had been purchased for conversion into a church. Standing behind the pulpit, I had a vision.

I could see myself attending a party, but it was a party at which I did not know anyone else in the room. In my vision, I walked out the back door and away from the party. It seemed significant to me that there were three steps that I had to descend to get out the door.

After descending the steps in my vision, I saw a pathway. I started to follow it, but there was a thick fog rising from the ground just like the fog I had experienced while fighting the Japanese in the Philippine Islands during World War II.

I remember thinking that if I was going to walk farther along that pathway, then I had to go by faith. It was then that I realized that everyone from the party was quietly following behind me.

I knew from my vision that if I dragged my feet, then those following behind would be able to sense my doubt. I was determined to walk with confidence wherever I thought the path might lead us. The people continued to follow me silently in the vision. Suddenly, I sensed that I had fallen off of a slight overhang and into a pool of water.

There was no time to warn my followers. The people behind me began tumbling into the water after me. I remembered having been a lifeguard and the training from my Navy days came back also. I tried to swim ashore so that I could rescue all of them.

Gradually I realized that there were too many drowning people foundering in the water. I then noticed a single man standing on the shore. He was holding out towards me what appeared to be a large timber with a crosspiece attached. All I had to do was help the people get hold of the timber. That was how we could all make it out of the water alive. That is, as long as the bearded man standing on the shore held fast to his end of the timber.

I stayed in the water until the very last of those people who had tumbled into the water after me had been saved. The man on shore still stood, holding out the timber for me. That is the moment I realized it was the Lord Jesus who was holding onto the cross. He was stretching it out for all who needed it. I also realized that it was my job to help the people around me grab hold of the cross.

With that realization, my vision ended. I was still standing beside the pulpit in the very house we were starting to use as a church. Naturally, I spent quite a bit of time trying to fathom the full depth of my vision.

From that day forward, some forty years later, I have never again considered quitting the ministry. I realized then as I do today that the devil himself had tried to get me to leave the ministry. But the Holy Spirit provided me with the vision and the strength that I needed so desperately in order to continue on with God's work.

CHAPTER THIRTY

MERGING PRESBYTERIANS AND BAPTISTS

After organizing the new church in Leggett, I continued to preach there while at the same time exploring the possibility of starting a second new church in nearby Laytonville. The two churches would make a nice two-point mission field since neither congregation was large enough to support a full-time minister on its own. The chairman of the Presbytery's committee on missions contacted me and asked me if I could take a look at a church in Covelo, another town just east of Leggett. I was to report back to the committee with my assessment whether the Covelo church should be dissolved or left to struggle.

That was about the same time that I received a second call, this one from Dr. J. Earl Jackman, who at that time was head of the Presbyterian Church's Board of National Missions. Earl Jackman called me and told me that he, too, had been contacted about the Covelo church. He wanted me to visit there on his behalf, and report back both to Presbytery and to him.

Summer was fast approaching, so I went to Covelo thinking that I would lead a vacation Bible school. What I found when I arrived were two church buildings, one Presbyterian and other Baptist, situated directly across the street from each other.

Many churches still used wood-burning heaters in those days, and they weren't always kept in the best repair. Often, the older churches would burn down from time to time. Apparently, this had happened so frequently that the two congregations just across the road from each other would share facilities until the other congregation could rebuild. Finally, the two congregations merged to form a single body of believers under the Baptist church roof. But they still had members who identified themselves as either Presbyterian or Baptist, and that created plenty of friction that drove people away in ever increasing numbers over the years. Finally, the church could no longer afford its own minister, so the Presbytery had supplied interim pastors for the last few years.

It was not difficult for me to discover the many reasons why the Covelo church was functioning so poorly. But much to my utter amazement, I discovered two older men who faithfully went alone down to the Presbyterian Church's building every Sunday morning. There, they would build a fire to provide a bit of warmth as they read the Sunday newspaper together. At the end of their solitary fellowship time, the two men would pray fervently and long THAT THE COVELO PRESBYTERIAN CHURCH WOULD RISE UP AGAIN!

The Baptist church across the road had been used for a church school in the past. But now, it also stood vacant.

After taking stock of the situation, I made my decision. What else could I do? I felt called by God to bring that Covelo church back from the brink of destruction. I began by visiting each of the families residing in the valley. Soon, I announced my intentions to lead a vacation Bible school that same summer.

I also talked with each of the families that had left the church for one reason or another. Many of them indicated to me that they were interested in bringing back the Presbyterian Church. The minister from the local Pentecostal Assembly of God congregation also unwittingly helped our cause. Since many of the families previously associated with the Presbyterian Church were sending their children to Sunday school classes at the Assembly of God church, the Pentecostal pastor challenged the young people to draw pictures of how their parents were being used by the devil.

Merging Presbyterians and Baptists

I was not assigned as the organizing pastor, but the Holy Spirit and I resurrected that Covelo church together. Since the Baptist Church building was in better condition than the Presbyterian Church building, I wrote to every Baptist conference for which I could find an address. They all denied any ownership in the structure.

As a result, lawyers in San Francisco who had been hired by the Presbytery were able to get title to both church buildings under the name of a newly reorganized Presbyterian Church of Covelo. Those families who had been raised in the old Presbyterian Church, as well as many others, came to attend services in the new Covelo Presbyterian Church.

Truly, the Lord works in wonderful ways.

CHAPTER THIRTY-ONE
A SERPENT IN THE GARDEN OF EDEN

Following the Covelo Church assignment, the Presbyterian Church's Board of National Missions asked me to undertake yet another very unusual experiment. This time they wanted to plant a politically active minister in a lower class area of San Jose's east side. This was an area predominantly populated with racial minorities. The experiment was to determine whether such a person could successfully attract enough people with which to raise a church congregation.

The plan involved my organizing a diverse group of politically active organizations—everything from homeowners associations to unions and management groups—into a community council. It was my intent to be so well known by those in power at city hall and in county government that I could develop some political clout.

The organizations grew politically powerful very quickly. But the large Presbyterian churches located on the wealthier west side of town began to oppose everything that we attempted.

One of our committee members learned that whenever any of San Jose's street sweeping equipment broke down, the east side of town was shorted of a cleaning day. However, residents on the west side of town continued to have their streets cleaned on an uninterrupted schedule.

That was fairly easy for us to verify since most of the city's street sweeper drivers actually lived on the east side of town.

We fought that inequality.

We also fought for fluoridation of the city's drinking water because children living on the east side of town desperately needed it. Residents on the west side apparently thought they did not need fluoridated water because they could afford regular fluoride treatments at the dentist. They did not want to be taxed for the needs of the poorer east side residents who could not afford regular dental care.

But mostly we fought for racial equality.

One of the demonstrations we sponsored was at an apartment complex on the west side. The apartment complex was named The Garden of Eden. It had a wall all the way around it. And it also had a security gate. We started informational picketing outside The Garden of Eden after an engineer—a graduate of CAL-Berkeley who had recently been hired by a firm in the Silicon Valley area near San Jose—was denied residence there.

It seems that the engineer had a white friend living in The Garden of Eden who had told him of a vacancy. But when the engineer, who was Asian, applied for occupancy he was refused. The engineer then hired a white man to successfully rent an apartment on his behalf. Shortly after the Asian engineer moved in, he was told he would have to vacate his apartment immediately because it had been deemed unsafe and the owners wanted to renovate it.

At that point, the engineer came to us and we scheduled a big demonstration. As I remember, nearly a hundred people turned out to picket on the first day. An artist friend of mine made a large sign with a snake painted on it. The sign also had these words, in large letters:

"There is a Serpent in the Garden of Eden." The letter "S" was formed by the snake's body.

I was wearing a black suit complete with a clerical collar when a news crew from one of the local television stations came to interview our group. Later that same day, there we all were on the 6 P.M. news. And this newscast was not just aired in San Jose. It had gone out all over the state of California.

A Serpent in the Garden of Eden

I learned later that a man in San Francisco was watching the news program and said to his wife,

"I think I own that Garden of Eden."

He then called his property manager and ordered his own people to identify the minister or priest who had appeared on the news show.

As it turned out, I received a telephone call from the property owner at about 10 P.M. that same day. He invited me to have lunch with him the following day and he suggested that we meet at the Top of the Mark. This restaurant, built on the top floor of the Mark Hopkins Hotel, was one of the fanciest places in all of San Francisco. I agreed to meet with him there. During our luncheon, he asked why our community organization was marching in protest outside of his apartment complex. After the engineer's story was related, the property owner ordered changes in the complex's rental requirements so that professional people of all races and others who could afford to live in the apartments would be included without discrimination.

That was one experience in which I can honestly say that the Holy Spirit broke the color line in San Jose.

Other victories soon followed suit.

But I eventually left San Jose unhappy with many of the blacks who were so quick to complain about the lack of help in their own fights for racial inequality, but would not, in their turn, help a neighbor suffering from a similar injustice. Just as quickly as those blacks were liberated, they became what I referred to as coconuts.

They were brown on the outside, but they acted white on the inside. They could not be bothered to help other blacks still living in the ghettos. I mistakenly counted on them as workers of the Lord who would reach out to help their own people and others.

CHAPTER THIRTY-TWO
DR. JAMES EARL JACKMAN RIDES TO MY RESCUE

Eventually, and primarily due to political pressure from churches on the west side of San Jose, the local missions committee of Presbytery voted to terminate the San Jose project experiment.

However, the project was in actuality a missions endeavor of the National Board of Missions. I do not believe the local Presbytery and Synod leaders realized what would happen as a result of their decision until later when they went to New York City seeking annual allocations for their own mission projects from the national board.

In New York City, my friend and mentor, Dr. J. Earl Jackman, took each of them aside and told them in no uncertain words that if they tried to remove me from the San Jose project then their local mission budget would be history. Earl Jackman was one of the most successful fund-raisers that the Board of National Missions ever had. He always wore the fanciest of suits and conducted himself as a real gentleman. But most all the pastors and church leaders knew that you didn't dare cross him either. He never forgot anything. If someone tried to take away funding for one of his favorite programs, with just one or two words, he could strip an entire Presbytery of half of its annual mission funding provided by the national church.

I think you can guess what the Presbytery committee members did next.

They reversed their previous action.

It seems that since I was part of a national headquarters project funded out of New York, the only action Presbytery could take was to bring morals charges against me, or suspend me for something along those same lines. But they never did that, primarily because I believe they were too afraid of losing their local missions budget.

However, they did put out the word to leaders about town that I was history. It was widely known that the moneyed west side churches had done their best to oust me. It seemed to many people that my days in San Jose were numbered.

Men from the local union hall were among the first to invite me to lunch. They wanted me to consider working as a union organizer for the labor council if my church job was lost. They remembered that I had been a member in good standing of the American Federation of Machinists while attending seminary and operating the mobile mechanic repair business on evenings and weekends. They had already taken steps, they informed me, to restore my membership in my former local so I could legally be employed as an organizer. That way, they figured, I could still continue to serve on the community council.

Even though they offered me a large salary, I told them I could not be tempted.

I had organized so many groups into the community council. Each time I did so, I heard complaint after complaint about the west side churches and how they dominated the local council of churches. Ministers from the west side of San Jose filled all positions on the governing board of the local council of churches. Whenever a speaker was chosen for the community celebrations on various holy days, it was always a minister from the west side of town who got the assignment. So I began to organize an alternative council of churches for the congregations on the east side of San Jose. It was a task for more than one person. I needed some help, so I went seeking assistance from the evangelical churches as well as the main line churches.

Vatican II, an ecumenical movement led by the Catholic Church, had recently been announced in Rome. I wanted to include the

Dr. James Earl Jackman Rides to My Rescue

Roman Catholic churches as well as a mission of theirs. When it came to electing the first president of the east side council of churches, the evangelicals did not want a fight to ensue between themselves and the main line churches. So they nominated me and insisted that I become the council's first president.

An Episcopal priest had made it widely known that he wanted to be the first president. I was convinced that he would perform the job very well. When the evangelical churches nominated me despite my objections, I voted for the Episcopal priest.

However, he received only two votes. Mine, and—I can only assume—his own.

After the vote was announced, the various council members started to leave. I asked one of the Baptist ministers why they had elected me. He indicated that it was because I had a foot in both camps. I was known as a Bible believing conservative, but I was also a member of a major denomination. The council was made up of ministers, priests and lay leaders from almost all of the churches on the entire east side of San Jose.

When the Roman Catholics heard that I had been ousted by the west side churches, I was invited to lunch by two priests with whom I was very close. They also invited a Jesuit from Santa Clara. During our luncheon, they offered me an opportunity to become a Jesuit. They desperately wanted me to continue working with the community council and to lead the various political action groups. All that was necessary was for me to sign a piece of paper stating that I would no longer sleep with my wife. They offered me a mathematics teaching assignment at the University of Santa Clara. They even hinted that the "wife thing" could eventually be, in their words, worked out.

Except for the "wife thing," I was tempted.

The politics of the Presbyterian Church was beginning to disgust me. I wanted to leave San Jose. I strongly believed that in three years we had failed to prove the viability of the experiment's thesis: That a highly visible, politically active minister would automatically be able to gather up and grow a church congregation.

Eventually, I received a visit from the two PhDs who had conceived the experiment for the Presbyterian Church's National Board of Missions. They both encouraged me to stay on in the area and run for political office.

But I was done with their experiment. And I told them so!

CHAPTER THIRTY-THREE
HELL'S ANGELS AND HOT DOGS

One of the wildest things that happened during my tenure in San Jose was the interest we attracted from the local Hell's Angels motorcycle club. I was invited to attend one of their meetings, to make a presentation on community action, and explain to the club's members how they could have an effective politically active presence.

As the club president introduced me, I stood up to speak dressed in my cleric's collar. Many of the club's members, and they were all of them dressed in black leather jackets, started to laugh out loud at me. They called me terrible things and swore continuously at me in really loud voices.

At that point, the club president, a man by the name of Big John, stood up and in the same motion slapped his hand down hard on the table top beside him.

"SILENCE! The Reverend is here because I invited him. I believe we need some political clout, so listen!" Big John shouted out at full volume.

"The next guy to pop off, I'll personally break his head," he continued.

Big John was aptly named. He stood about 6-feet, 11-inches, and weighed well over 300 pounds. He had a powerful presence, and his voice was loud even when he spoke softly. When he shouted, the volume was almost deafening.

Dead silence engulfed me as I explained how all participating groups on the community council were required to assist each other whenever any of the partnering groups scheduled political confrontations. Following my presentation, the Hell's Angels club members voted to join with us. During my entire tenure on the community council, the motorcycle club was always represented at every march or demonstration even though the requirement was group participation in only two of every three political actions.

While in San Jose, I also remember one amusing mistake I made.

Languages have always been easy for me so I quickly began to pick up a little street Spanish. After a few months, I could understand what was said to me, and I could speak enough words to make my wishes known.

One day, we decided to do a promotion for the Little League baseball teams in the Mexican section of town. This was then known as the barrio of Salis Tu Puedes (Rise Up and Walk), but which the barrio residents loosely translated as "Get Out If You Can." At the fund-raiser, we sold a hot dog and a soft drink for just 10 cents. Armour Star Meats, the Wonder Bread bakery, and local Coca-Cola bottlers donated the food and drink items to our committee at no cost.

I set up a public address system that I owned, then left the work to others as I was scheduled to help at a huge trading table set up at the nearby Pink Elephant flea market. Other duties kept me away from the barrio for several hours.

Upon my return, I found the parking lot jammed and hundreds of people scurrying around. But I could not hear anyone using the public address system to tell members of the crowd where they could eat for almost nothing. I walked over to the platform and encouraged the event organizers to use the public address system.

Their response was they were afraid to talk into the microphone, so I picked it up and started to speak. Before I said anything in Spanish, I turned to Raul, a friend of mine who was a college graduate.

"How do you say it?" I inquired

Raul just shrugged his shoulders, so I began on my own.

Hell's Angels and Hot Dogs

"Perro Caliente, Diez Centavos!" I said into the microphone

Derisive laughter and plenty of snickers greeted my voice. My friend Maria fell over in a faint. No one corrected me, so I continued to repeat my sales pitch in Spanish many more times.

It was some months later that I finally learned what everyone had been laughing about. While it is true that the Spanish word for dog is "perro" and "caliente" means hot, the slang terms I was using meant something entirely different to those Mexican Americans. It seems that I was announcing the sale of a young girl in heat—one dressed to seduce—for the paltry price of 10 cents.

Regardless of the message, we sold so many hot dogs that day that none of us could believe our success.

Another humorous incident revolved around my habit of wearing a clerical collar so that I wouldn't be mistaken for a door-to-door salesman.

This happened while I was visiting in a San Jose hospital just before a friend's surgery. We had a short prayer, and then, because it was 6 A.M. and I had not yet eaten, I went down to the hospital's cafeteria for breakfast while I waited until my friend was out of the recovery room.

To pass the time, I was looking at the front page of that morning's San Jose Mercury News on display in the newspaper vending machine. I was trying to decide whether to purchase a copy when I heard a commotion a short distance away. Taking a few steps down a nearby ramp, I found myself facing the hospital's emergency entrance. There, by the double doors, I saw two men waving their arms and calling out to me.

Still preoccupied with the dilemma of whether to invest a quarter for a morning newspaper, I did not fully understand what it was they wanted of me. The two men eventually approached me still gesturing, until finally each of the men grabbed one of my arms and propelled me—almost carried me—back down the ramp towards the emergency entrance.

"Father! He's dying," said one of them who was in obvious anguish.

"But I'm not a Catholic priest," I tried to explain, even as I knew my protestations were falling on deaf ears.

They rushed me past some curtains and into an emergency treatment room where I saw on the hospital gurney an Italian man whose body was rapidly turning from gray to blue. He was still alive, but just barely. Standing beside him was a matronly woman whom I presumed to be the dying man's wife of many years.

I realized quickly that the only Christian thing to do at that moment was to give the dying man his last rites. That I attempted to do, even though my Latin was not the best. Instead, I mumbled the half-remembered words as I made the sign of the cross over the dying man's eyes, ears and mouth. By the time I reached his hands, I perceived that he was most likely already dead. But I continued to bless his feet as well, and whispered into his ear encouraging him to make a good confession. I then bent my head to place my ear next to his motionless mouth.

I don't remember now whether he actually said anything to me. But I do remember seeing the faces of his wife and the two ambulance attendants who had rushed me to his bedside. They were all just beaming. They looked so pleased that I couldn't bear to let their spirits down.

Afterwards, the wife asked me to which parish I belonged. Automatically, I started to reach into my pocket for a business card, but then reconsidered. My mind focused on my Roman Catholic friend, Father Tom, who was organizing a new parish in the south part of San Jose.

"Santa Maria Goretti," I then told her as she thanked me profusely.

Upon returning home, I immediately telephoned my friend, Father Tom, and told him what had just happened. He thanked me as well.

Weeks later, Father Tom telephoned to let me know that the widow had sent in a contribution, and it was one of the biggest checks the Catholic priest had ever received. Accompanying the twenty-thousand-dollar-check was a case of wine. Apparently, I had conferred last rites on one of the oldest and wealthiest wine growers in the entire county.

Father Tom gave me the case of wine as a token of the widow's gratitude for my services. But we both agreed that his parish should keep the widow's entire check.

These are just some of the many wonderful memories I have carried with me throughout my ministry.

CHAPTER THIRTY-FOUR
DISADVANTAGES OF BEING CLERGY

Although I enjoyed most of the experiences associated with my calling to the ministry, I must admit that there are also certain disadvantages associated with being a member of the clergy.

The first example of this occurred when a dear friend, Irene Davis, died in San Jose. Although Eulalie and I were now living in Redding, we had both become acquainted with the Davis family while I was working for three years with churches and organizing community groups in east San Jose. Irene Davis had served faithfully as bookkeeper for the community group association.

At the time Mrs. Davis died, her daughter called to let me know the time and date of her mother's funeral. I was also given the name of a funeral home where an evening viewing was to be held one day before the funeral. At least, I thought I had the facts straight!

My wife and I left Redding on the morning of the viewing and we had a relaxed four-hour drive to San Jose. We located a motel, then I looked up the mortuary's number in the local phone book. It was past 5 P.M. when the mortuary chain's branch office in Milpitas finally answered my call. The person on the other end gave me detailed directions on how to reach the mortuary, and I easily found the place moments later.

I went to the door and fully expected family members to already be there as 5:30 P.M. was the time that the family was supposed to gather for viewing of the open casket. Instead a young man met me at the mortuary door. I introduced myself as the Rev. Clifford Baker, and then I asked politely if we could join the family of Irene Davis.

All right, he said, then disappeared to make a phone call. Upon his return, he again questioned me at length as to who I was and which family was I there to see. I once again explained that I had been called by Irene Davis' daughter Judy, that I was a friend of the family, and a member of the clergy who lived in Redding, Calif.

I was very confused by all of these delays and by this man's formal line of questioning. All that he would divulge to me was that Irene's remains were not at the Milpitas mortuary. Once again, he excused himself and remained for some time talking with someone on the telephone. When he re-emerged, he informed me that he had just talked with Judy, who was now at home.

It seems that the family had gathered at the San Jose branch of the mortuary earlier in the evening, at the time I had been given, and then returned to their various homes.

The young man from the Milpitas mortuary branch then asked me: "Who told you that you would be performing services for Mrs. Davis?"

I responded that I never told anyone that I was to perform the service. I merely was an old friend of the family who came to be with them in their time of need.

From his surprised response, I immediately realized where the confusion arose. When I initially called the Milpitas office, I introduced myself as the Rev. Clifford Baker. The attendant who answered the telephone must have assumed that I was intending to conduct the services. He had checked with another branch in downtown San Jose and discovered that a different minister was actually scheduled to perform the burial and memorial services the following day. Thinking that he was protecting the family from any unpleasantness, he had merely directed me out to the Milpitas branch and away from the San Jose viewing, which by that time we had missed completely.

Disadvantages of Being Clergy

However, once the confusion was unraveled, Eulalie and I did make it to the memorial and graveside services the following day. We stayed for the reception afterwards, met with all of Mrs. Davis's children, and we were even invited to a family get-together at Irene's home following the funeral. All's well that ends well is all I will say.

Another incident providing testimony that the life of a minister is not all roses occurred in 1971 when the brother-in-law of my son Arthur was to be married in Central Point, Oregon. The bride's father, who was also a minister, had called to ask if I would assist him in the wedding ceremony. Everything was arranged by telephone. He was a Pentecostal minister who was serving an independent church. Although he would conduct the actual vows, he needed someone to run the service up through the point where he would walk with the bride—his daughter—down the center aisle.

I was to conduct the service up until the part where I would ask: "Who gives this woman to be married to this man?"

He would answer, "Her mother and I do."

Then, instead of taking his seat, he would come forward and perform the remainder of the ceremony.

Well, on the day of the wedding, I arrived at the church dressed in my standard clerical garb: Black suit and black vest with a clerical collar. For many years, this had been my daily uniform. But as I reached the steps to the church, I found the doorway blocked by a large, big-boned woman who stood fully in my way with her arms folded.

"Father, you have the wrong church!" she said to me in a challenging tone. "The church you want is across town."

"But I am here to assist in the wedding service for the pastor of this church, or at least I think so," I replied, wondering if once again I had managed to mix up the directions.

"Over my dead body!" she responded.

We stared at each other silently for a few moments as I pondered the situation. Then it dawned on me. She was mistaking me for a Catholic priest. Handing her my business card, I requested that she present it to the church's pastor, who—I added—was expecting me. She took one look at the card.

"So you're a Presbyterian minister?" she said.

"Do all of you go around looking like Catholic priests?" the woman continued.

"No," I responded. "But maybe after the service, if you and I have some time, I will explain why I wear these clothes."

"That should be very interesting," she replied, continuing with a haughty tone.

At the end of the wedding ceremony, I did get an opportunity to tell her the following story which explains why I usually wear a clerical collar.

During the period that I was organizing churches and community groups in east San Jose, I often went door to door looking for families who might be interested in forming a new church. A lot of doors were slammed in my face, but I continued on in faith.

One day, I knocked on a door answered by a very nice woman.

"You're a minister?" she wanted to know. "You are just the answer to my prayers."

She then told me about a woman who lived across the fence from her who apparently was having a terrible time. She needs to speak with a minister, my hostess explained. As she was relaying this information, she was also escorting me out her back door and across the yard until we came face to face with a second woman. This one I instantly recognized as one of those who had previously slammed a door in my face without saying a single word.

"Why didn't you tell me that you were a minister?" she asked me accusingly once we were introduced.

I decided to just let her comment pass while I listened for quite some time as she recounted her many troubles and ailments.

Following that incident, I concluded never to be mistaken for another door-to-door salesman. For the remainder of my ministry, I was never again taken to be a solicitor, although several times I was thought to be a Catholic priest.

CHAPTER THIRTY-FIVE

THE CELLAR

Shortly after the San Jose experiment ended, Dr. James Earl Jackman telephoned to ask me whether I would be interested in attempting to merge two struggling churches that had the ability to be financially independent only if they joined congregations. It was hoped that eventually the two churches would be able to build a central building to serve the combined membership.

My investigation revealed that the two churches were only a couple of miles apart and they already shared a minister. The area between the two towns had long since been settled by business and professional people. Each of the struggling churches had originally been organized in the horse and buggy days when there was a greater distance—at least in time traveled—between them.

The biggest obstacle to the merger was that each of the churches ran short of money at the end of every year. In order to make it through the year financially, they continuously applied for emergency mission funding to fill the gaps. My father-in-law spoke to some of the elders he knew there. Eventually, I was offered the two-point field on the Long Beach peninsula in southwestern Washington state. This was once again a task that had been turned down by several other ministers prior to my call there.

From a Speakeasy to the Cross

The local Presbytery wanted a strong man to unify the two churches. I moved there and within three years, using a lot of my own brute strength mixed with more than a bit of awkwardness, the Holy Spirit blended them together. During my time there, I also raised a substantial building fund for construction of a unified church facility. Naturally, there were those unhappy with my power broker tactics. But I launched a popular youth program in the basement of the Ilwaco church. We called it The Cellar and the teenagers flocked to it on weekends.

After three years, I figured my job was completed in merging those two churches. Truthfully, neither I nor my family cared much for the place, so I began to look around for a new calling.

CHAPTER THIRTY-SIX

MILLWRIGHT CARPENTER

That was when Paul Friday called me from the small church in McCloud, California. I was familiar with the area. Geographically it was in close proximity and very similar sociologically to the lumber camps and mill town communities in which I had conducted my tent evangelism while residing in Big Bend and Redding. I tried to stall, and asked Paul Friday if the church pastor seeking committee was considering any other pastoral candidates.

Paul Friday called me again about a week later. He said the church's pastor seeking committee had indeed extended a call to another man who at first seemed interested in the position, but in the end had turned it down.

That was the sign that I was seeking.

I never accepted a call unless it had first been declined by someone else. The church in McCloud and I bonded so well that I stayed in that job nearly 15 years.

I arrived in town shortly after the McCloud River Lumber Company had sold the sawmill along with much of the town. In the heyday of logging and sawmill operations, the more successful lumber companies purchased all of the land surrounding a permanent mill site, and then built a town to grow up around it. In McCloud, the lumber company owned all of the houses, most of the stores, one or two of the hotels, and even the church building.

The church was seventy-five years old and during all those years passed, the company had paid the church's utilities as well as one-half of the minister's salary. Now that the sawmill had been sold to outside investors, the utility and salary supplements were discontinued. I found myself serving a very small congregation in a town where more than 70 percent of the town's occupants had Italian surnames and who were most likely not about to attend a Protestant church. The congregation I had been called to serve could not afford to pay the annual heating bill, let alone provide a minister with a salary.

After about a year of struggling to live on the meager salary the church did pay, I decided to find employment at the mill even as I continued to work half-time at the church. While I was in seminary, I had often dreamed of being a tent evangelist, or as the Apostle Paul called it in his writings, a tent maker. This was now my opportunity.

According to Paul, being a tent maker means serving a church while working on the outside as well. I started working at the mill at the very bottom rung. I was the night shift cleanup man. Within two years I had worked myself up to a position as millwright carpenter, and I was also a relief planerman. This presented me with a moral dilemma.

Throughout my ministry, I was determined not to ever place myself in a competitive position in terms of salary. But at the sawmill, I now held one of the most highly sought after and better-paying positions in the planing mill.

It was only after a great deal of prayer that I finally came to terms with it all. In the end, I decided that it must be the Lord's will, since there were quite a few additional expenses now that our three children—Arthur, Charlotte and young Beth—were then attending high school and college.

CHAPTER THIRTY-SEVEN
THE HOLY SPIRIT ALWAYS FINDS A WAY

During the first three years that I worked in the mill, I was the object of a fair amount of good-natured kidding and the butt of more than a few jokes. The non-Christian men working in the sawmill would pronounce the word "preacher" like it was something that belonged in a toilet. Throughout it all, I just tolerated their derision and hoped that someday, and certainly only with assistance from the Holy Spirit, I would be taken into their confidence. Towards the end of my third year working in the mill, I began to despair that there would never be a miracle from the Holy Spirit that would open up a ministry to those men.

But looking back, it was only after I had endured those three years with little or no opportunity to counsel or help lead the men to Christ that a strange thing happened.

One day, the lunch whistle blew and I started heading toward the bicycle that took me all over town. Another planerman stepped out into the area where all of us exited the building and through which the finished lumber was also hauled. He commenced to cuss me up and down something terrible.

I was stunned!

Apparently, so were the other men who were leaving.

I started back towards him with the intention of knocking him on his butt except that when I reached him, the Holy Spirit got to me first. So I just grabbed him by the shirt and forced him to sit down in a nearby chair.

"What the hell is bugging you, Jim?" I asked him. "I can tell that something is eating at your gut!"

Well, he began to tell me how his wife was leaving him, and his daughter had been sleeping with some good-for-nothing man. Finally, Jim said to me that it just seemed as if he couldn't do anything about either of those problems. At that point, he broke down and started to cry.

I spent my whole lunch hour talking with him, counseling him and quoting scripture to him. Later, I visited several times with him and his family in the nearby town of Mount Shasta. We were eventually able, by working together, to help him solve many of the problems plaguing his family life.

That incident opened up a floodgate of opportunities for me as a minister. Almost every day, one or another of the men I worked with would come to me to talk over their problems. This happened not just at breaks or lunch time, but while I was repairing steps, working on replacing floorboards, or fixing a section of hand railing.

One of my friends, a Seventh Day Adventist and a real Christian who had never been involved in teasing me, worked with me on the mill construction crew. One day while we were working together, I casually mentioned to him that some of the men had sought me out for counseling.

"I know," he said.

It was a mystery how he could know that as he did not work with me in the planing mill area where most of these contacts had taken place. He said that during the past three years, he overheard many of the men talking about me. His explanation led me to understand why it had taken so long for me to gain their confidence

Apparently, he said, since I was working days at the mill and would often use my nights to go calling on the men living in the town, everyone had been watching me. They would call each other on the telephone to check and see whether I was having any affairs with the wives of men who were working a night shift.

The Holy Spirit Always Finds a Way

They compared notes to see whether I was actually visiting the men, or was I visiting women who were alone at home. The men would keep track whether the shades were drawn after I arrived, or whether the lights came on in the bedrooms of the homes I visited.

I was so shocked I just sat there in silence.

My friend then told me that in the town's long and colorful history, there had been all sorts of "preachers" who had come to work in the mill. They would go around at night visiting homes while the man was at work. All the signs of an affair were evident. Those so-called preachers were soon on their way out of town carrying with them all of the money they had raised in donations for one charity after another.

I told my friend that I was shocked and surprised to have been lumped together with those other pseudo ministers.

That isn't, by any stretch of the imagination, to imply that I didn't make my share of mistakes.

During one labor cutback at the sawmill, I took a temporary job operating the hog mill. A mechanical problem halted operations of the conveyor belt that carried the unusable log trimmings to the hog, which is a machine that makes chips out of the trimmings.

The chips are then burned in a large furnace that provides steam power throughout the sawmill. With the conveyor shut down, there was little that the rest of us could do.

Now, I had repeatedly warned one of the men at least a dozen times that he was not to throw anything onto the conveyor belt when it wasn't running because it might bring harm to the hog operator working down below.

Well, of course he threw some wood trimmings down the hole and they bruised my arm. I walked upstairs to the main floor of the sawmill and commenced to knock him on his butt with one punch. Then, I threw some wood trims on him so he could see whether he liked the feeling. He reported me to the foreman and, as a result, I was suspended from work for three days.

I was wrong and so I apologized to him.

No one else seemed to hold that incident against me. But I always felt guilty about having done it.

CHAPTER THIRTY-EIGHT
THE MILL BIBLE

When the new translation of the Living Bible came out, I received a free paperback copy from the publisher. So I took it to the mill and placed it in my locker. It wasn't long before a small group of men would gather together at lunch time for a Bible study. This group met off and on, but at least it was a beginning.

The Bible that remained in my locker became a symbol to me of the changes taking place in the men. A "hippie" who worked behind the re-saw was one of the first to go to my locker, take out the Bible, and share some passage with another workmen who apparently disagreed with him about what the good book said.

That would soon become a common occurrence. I found out how frequently the Bible was being used by the others quite by accident one day when I was eating lunch at a different time than usual. I had taken the Bible out of my locker for something to read. One of the other men came into the lunchroom and said to me,

"So you've got the Mill Bible," he said to me. "I couldn't find it. Give it here! Bill doesn't believe that it says Jesus just called Lazarus from out of the tomb."

I had never before heard anyone refer to the Bible I kept in my locker as the "Mill Bible." Suddenly, it became clear to me how the Bible was getting to be so soiled. I can remember times when the men would begin arguing over a particular passage. They would begin swearing until one of them would usually throw the Bible onto the sawmill floor. It was gratifying to me to see the Mill Bible speaking out so loudly to so many men.

Cutline info: The Mill Bible that the Rev. Clifford Baker kept for many years in his locker at the sawmill in McCloud.

The Mill Bible

Like all good things that must finally end, I contracted heart trouble and had to quit working at the mill. About that same time, the sawmill also closed down.

Along with both of these events, my ministry to those men ended.

What happened to the man I knocked down for throwing trimmings down the hog hole? We became friends. He came over to my house to see me many times during the years that followed. And what about the first man to break the silence and cuss me out before he could finally talk about his problems? He and his entire family came to the hospital to visit me when I had the heart attack that finally ended my ministry in McCloud.

Today, the Mill Bible remains in my possession. I cherish it, dirty pages and all.

After all, those finger marks were made by men who at least took the time and effort to read God's Word. I take comfort in knowing, as the years went on, that some of them eventually confessed Jesus as their own Lord and Savior.

CHAPTER THIRTY-NINE
MCCLOUD CENTENNIAL

In May of 2005, I made a return pilgrimage to the Presbyterian Church in McCloud, where I had served for 14 years prior to my retirement.

Organized originally in 1905, the McCloud church was celebrating its 100th anniversary. As the weekend celebration began on a Friday night, ministers and laymen from several other churches in a twelve-mile area began to gather. While visiting with those in attendance, I eventually recognized the Baptist minister and made my way through the assembled crowd to share a word with him. Standing next to him was a tall fellow whom at first I did not recognize. But when the young man finally came over to me, he said, "Cliff, I was hoping that you would be here."

I still didn't know who he might be until he introduced himself as Randy Halkyard. The name sounded familiar, but I still couldn't place the face or how we might have come to meet prior to this celebration. He explained that he was just a teenager when I had arrived in McCloud to start my ministry there. Like many of the town's young people, he had been fooling around with drugs and alcohol. He told me that so many people in that town were mean to him and put him down, but I had never treated him that way.

Randy and I spent some time reminiscing about the youth program that we started in the McCloud Church's social hall. I told him that while serving a two-point parish in Ilwaco, Wash., we had a successful youth program in the church basement that we renamed The Cellar, so naturally I wanted to bring that same experience to McCloud.

At the McCloud church, however, the social hall was much larger. But whenever we moved aside the chairs and tables so the young people could take part in activities and games, the older ladies of the church would raise a fuss. As a result, the teen's gathering room in McCloud was quickly dubbed Granny's Pad and we were always careful to return all the furniture to its original location when cleaning up.

We were successful, Randy and I remembered, because the church provided a decent place where the teenagers could bring their musical instruments, set them up on a stage, and play the night away. The church even provided soft drinks. I reminded Randy that the ladies of the church also made lemonade by the bucket-full. Our only rule, there was to be no alcohol or drugs!

"The first time I attended a function in Granny's Pad, I came in just knowing you would throw me out with insults," Randy told me. "But you treated me as if I was a decent person. I'll always remember that first night."

Later that same evening I learned that Randy had been saved some years back, and was currently a staunch member of the Baptist Church in McCloud.

END

To order additional copies of

FROM A SPEAKEASY
TO THE CROSS

Have your credit card ready and call:

1-877-421-READ (7323)

or please visit our web site at
www.pleasantword.com

Also available at:
www.amazon.com
and
www.barnesandnoble.com

Printed in the United States
55948LVS00003B/211